Praise for *Leading Giants*

"At 19 years old, my life changed forever when I was mentored by a true leader—a *Giant*, someone who had strength of character beyond the norm, was committed to self-mastery, and had developed extraordinary leadership abilities that enabled him to bring out the best in every person he led. In *Leading Giants*, Dave Durand will show you how to become that type of leader—a Giant who is capable of leading other Giants."

—Hal Elrod, International Bestselling Author,
The Miracle Morning Updated and Expanded Edition

"This book provides powerful and practical advice relevant to the challenges facing leaders in today's culture. In *Leading Giants*, Dave Durand covers the landscape of topics from value-based leadership to successfully building a healthy culture for your team and much more. This book will not disappoint."

—Thomas S. Monaghan, Founder, Domino's Pizza,
and Founder, Ave Maria University

"*Leading Giants* summarizes 30+ years of leadership training and development. Dave provides profound insights grounded in timeless principles that can transform your everyday life. His book is a recipe for becoming an exceptional leader and, more importantly, a guide to becoming a truly magnanimous person. Through engaging anecdotes and actionable advice, Dave inspires readers to cultivate habits of success, making this book an invaluable resource for personal and professional growth."

—Kevin O'Brien, CEO, Best Version Media

"Dave Durand not only lays out a plan to grow and lead your organization but also provides a road map to leading yourself. *Leading Giants* is an approachable book with big ideas."

—Rich Galgano, Founder and CEO, Windy City Wire,
and Managing Director, Carefree Capital

"Influence is the key to leadership. *Leading Giants* moves past the pollyanna approach used by many of today's 'influencers' and dives way into the core of true leadership. You can't give what you don't have. Dave shows you how to be the person worthy of leading true Giants. You've got to be a Giant to lead Giants."

—Joe Calloway, Bestselling Author, *Becoming a Category of One*

LEADING GIANTS

Also by Dave Durand

*Say It This Way: How to Build Trust and Motivate Others
with the Right Choice of Words*

*Perpetual Motivation: How to Light Your Fire and
Keep It Burning in Your Career and in Life*

Win the World Without Losing Your Soul

LEADING GIANTS

A Leader's Guide to Maximum Influence

DAVE DURAND

Matt Holt Books
An Imprint of BenBella Books, Inc.
Dallas, TX

Matt Holt is an imprint of BenBella Books, Inc.
8080 N. Central Expressway
Suite 1700
Dallas, TX 75206
benbellabooks.com
Send feedback to feedback@benbellabooks.com

BenBella and *Matt Holt* are federally registered trademarks.

Printed in the United States of America
10 9 8 7 6 5 4 3 2 1

Library of Congress Control Number: 2024033538
ISBN 9781637746332 (hardcover)
ISBN 9781637746349 (electronic)

Produced and Edited by Syris King-Klem LLC
Copyediting by Michael Fedison
Proofreading by Lisa Story
Text design and composition by PerfecType, Nashville, TN
Cover design by Brigid Pearson
Printed by Lake Book Manufacturing

Special discounts for bulk sales are available. Please contact bulkorders@benbellabooks.com.

CONTENTS

SECTION 3

Think Like a Criminal

INTRODUCTION

This is a book about building long-term greatness in yourself, your team, and your organization via the mastery of influence and proven leadership strategies. To a large degree, the words *leadership* and *influence* are interchangeable. Leadership can't be effective without influence and having influence almost always presents an opportunity to lead. I will commingle the words at times but also parse out some differences throughout the text. *Leading Giants* is the antidote to the perils of fleeting success, inconsistent influence, and the failure to build and lead great teams filled with high-powered people.

Most "leaders" are merely ineffective managers in a position of authority. They don't possess the traits that effective leaders have, so they can't influence others well. This book will show you how to become more effective, influential, and satisfied in your leadership role by becoming a Giant. *A Giant is someone who has strength of character beyond the norm, is committed to self-improvement, intoxicated by the discovery of truth, and compelled to help others become their best self.*

You must be a Giant to lead Giants, which takes deep resolve, but thankfully becoming a Giant is incredibly satisfying. People who find the greatest satisfaction and long-term effectiveness in their work know that **it's not so much what you do that matters, it's who you become when you do it** that matters most.

1

Whenever you try to do something the wrong way or with the wrong tools, it's either more difficult or impossible. *Leading Giants* is a guide to using the right tools to make leadership and influence easier. I begin by helping you form yourself with the crucial yet often missed virtues and habits that build greatness in leaders. I will break down high-level ideas into simple, usable forms to help you make better decisions, cultivate fairness, accelerate courage, and build self-control.

From there I will show you how to tap into the universal desires that 100% of us have so you can use them as fuel to inspire, influence, and lead others to greatness. I will continue with further ideas and practical strategies. Being a Giant is more of a journey than a destination, yet there are two things that define a Giant. The first is the decision to master virtue and simultaneously tame vice. This is what I call "virtue-based leadership," which is the discipline of establishing habits that guide a leader in making consistently good, effective, and moral decisions with relative ease. The second is doing the work necessary to accomplish that goal. A Giant is anyone who is on that path.

The more you master yourself, the bigger you become, until you see head and shoulders above the crowd. Once you are a Giant, you'll be drawn to leading other Giants. All leaders carry a unique burden. They are guardians, protectors, providers, judges, helpers, servants, counselors, and friends—and it takes a Giant to be all those at once. Unfortunately, the world sends confusing messages about leadership.

Movies and episodic shows, despite exaggerations, reflect real situations in our personal lives and the world at large. This is also true when it comes to how modern heroes and leaders are depicted. In fact, it's rare to see true heroes or good moral leaders in contemporary storytelling. In almost every popular show, the main characters are antiheroes. An antihero has as many bad traits as good traits, making the audience wonder how he or she will react in any given situation. This type of character makes things exciting and dramatic, which may attract a lot of viewers, but can send the wrong message. The classic antihero applies "values" whimsically, but through twists of fate and imaginative scriptwriting, they emerge the victor. Real life isn't that way.

Distinguishing between truly great leaders and antiheroes is important from the start. Anyone who specializes in training knows that undoing bad habits is sometimes as important as building good habits. True leaders have integrity, which is why they apply the same moral principles privately as they do publicly. They do the right thing because it is right, and they don't do the wrong thing because it's wrong. But antiheroes only think in terms of advancing their agenda. So, right and wrong are not true considerations for them. Goodness and truth are only used if it is convenient, which means lies are used more often. Over time, this weakens them until they have very little or no influence.

While I understand the nature of entertainment and the need to have high-contrast characters that entice people to the theater, to find what great leadership looks like, you're better off looking past the silver screen. All good leaders inevitably have flaws, but too often, people value vice and condemn virtue. Antiheroes are comfortable with their vices and have no real desire to change. Great leaders, on the other hand, rise above their flaws.

Antiheroes act like *nanos*, which is the Greek word for dwarf. These are people who exhibit behaviors that are opposite those of Giants. They act big but are vice laden and virtue deprived. As a result, they have less influence over time while Giants continue to grow their influence.

While I distinguish between antiheroes (nanos) and true heroes (Giants), I want to be clear that not all good leaders are "all good," and not all bad leaders are "all bad." We all have our vices and behaviors that are unhelpful, unproductive, or harmful. Therefore, this book offers guidance on how to be a great leader despite your shortcomings. Giants are not perfect all the time. The key here is to strive for perfection while understanding that you have shortcomings. This allows you to retain your own standards while having empathy for others who also fall short, just like you. Our shared human nature drives us to either build up or tear down. Even apathetic people slowly erode their character; therefore, we are all either growing or backsliding.

Understanding human nature sheds light on powerful strategies that are only possible through virtue. Human nature does not change as we age, although our understanding of it and how we respond to it does mature. That allows you to draw upon life experiences in varying circumstances to understand the context of situations seemingly unrelated. The virtue you will build in yourself and those you lead will create an orderly and therefore peaceful environment, even in relatively intense organizations. It is an axiom that you can't have peace without order, and you can't have prosperity without peace. Virtues are the gateway to that possibility because they are what build character muscles, which enable you to make great decisions, act fairly, move forward during difficulty, and control and direct passions.

Throughout the book I provide theory and philosophy in down-to-earth and usable ways, bolstered by practical applications and strategies. Understanding the "why" behind the how-to is essential so you can become a Giant, not just act like a Giant. If you've ever had the unfortunate experience of working for hours putting together a "some assembly required" item only to find that the last piece won't fit, you will understand why I want you to read it cover to cover. The reason the last piece won't fit is usually due to an earlier error that could have been avoided by paying closer attention to the instructions. Likewise, many of the problems we face inside our organizations are due to skipping important steps early on. I can't count the number of times I have been invited by leaders to "fix" their employees' bad attitudes or habits. This is a fool's errand. I never accept the challenge without being able to find out the root cause, which almost always starts with the leaders at the "top." Similarly, while it may be alluring to jump ahead to chapters that have the information you seek, keep in mind that the previous chapters hold essential strategies and nonnegotiable action items you must work on to have true success.

THEMES AND THROUGH LINES

As you read, you'll notice a few themes throughout this book. Among them is the idea that understanding human nature, virtue, and vice is paramount for leading Giants. I want to be clear that I am aware that there are many leaders who have built big companies with selective "values" and are basically antiheroes. You can certainly dictate, bully, and cheat your way to big things, but I would *not* call them successful. What's the wake left behind that organization? Did they ruin families, promote dangerous products, and defraud investors? Or did they provide great opportunities and make life better? Rarely is it one or the other, but the weight and impact of the good versus the bad often becomes the catalyst or the demise for a company's long-term results.

As I mentioned in the first paragraph, this is a book about building greatness in yourself, your team, and your organization via the mastery of influence and proven leadership strategies. With that, any and everything I propose in this book comes from insights that I either learned firsthand from failure or success or through the tremendous examples of my own mentors. I learned and applied them from guides who were true Giants in my life. I'm very lucky that so many insights were given to me through those Giants, such as my parents, mentors, and, beyond them, God's grace.

It took me 35 years of leading many organizations to gain the experience and insights needed to understand how to scale and lead organizations, and that learning process is not complete. Despite having had success, I am an eternal student to these topics—a pupil of the ever-unfolding layers that come from doing the work necessary to create something of good and true value in this world. It takes time to perfect the understanding required to maintain a healthy, sane, and thriving organizational culture. I chose to condense much of what I have learned over those years into one book that is easy to read and apply for the purpose of gaining immediate results. It is my hope that you accept the advice within these pages as an adventure.

On these pages you'll find the secrets to creating a thriving organizational culture and becoming a Giant who leads Giants. You'll gain the confidence to lead with conviction and humility, standing up for what you know is good, true, and beautiful. You'll experience the freedom that comes from doing difficult things in the face of all dysfunctions or opposition. You'll refine your ability to adapt, evolve, fine-tune, and appreciate what everyone brings to the table. Ultimately, you'll increase your productivity and prosperity but in a peaceful, empowered way. *But you'll only do any of this if you take action and implement the insights offered.* So, the end of each chapter has a section called "Giant Takeaways," which summarizes the chapter and gives you tools to make it real, make it last, and make it happen fast.

Leading Giants offers you a comprehensive guide for leading yourself and others to great success. Today more than ever, high-value businesses led by virtuous leaders are needed. You may or may not have your own business. You may be a manager, technician, or engineer who hasn't yet acted upon your entrepreneurial nudges, or you could be a leader of a massive global corporation. Regardless of your position within any given industry, what you're about to read will rapidly expand your influence and place you at the forefront of effective leadership. So, take courage, and know that you're not alone in the quest.

SECTION 1

The Four Superpowers
of a Leader

As a young entrepreneur I was very inspired by the most popular motivational experts of the day. Hearing them speak was like music to my ears. Any chance I got, I dove deeper and deeper into new books and audio lessons. I grew from what I read, and much of that information helped me lead my teams effectively, but there was something missing. So, I dug deeper and became certified in neuro-linguistic programming and in hypnotherapy (which, admittedly, was quite a dubious certification), and read hundreds of books. It seemed that, while there were many solid ideas, there was also too much complexity. Most ideas yielded temporary results. I wanted something that my team could use to strengthen themselves forever. I observed people who had long-term success, and I discovered they have several similar habits. I called them Legacy Achievers, and in 1998, I wrote a book about them called *Perpetual Motivation*. Today, I call them Giants. That book shares important insights about what this impressive group did, but as I matured, I noticed something more than just what they did that mattered.

I observed that many people in business think transactionally. They are motivated to have things, so they do activities to obtain the things they want to have. Whether it's power, money, or status, they know that if they do X, they can get Y. This is a good thing and a necessary starting place, but if that's as deep as you think, you remain mentally and morally shallow. You will fall short of becoming a Giant. A Giant asks, "Why do I want that?" or "Who will I become if I have it?" or "How will the way in which I go about getting it shape who I am?" I started to develop the important understanding that it is not what you do but who you become when you do things that matters. Then, like a lightning bolt, I learned of something that I couldn't believe I had never heard in the hundreds of motivational books I read or talks I listened to—virtue. Sure, an occasional mention of the word was hinted at here or there, but it was never discussed in depth. I began the grand adventure of learning how the great philosophers understood human nature. I was intoxicated by the works of Socrates, Aristotle, and Plato, then Saint Thomas Aquinas and more modern scholars. Since I was not and never will be a philosopher, I would not begin to say I understand their works to any degree that those educated in such fields do. However, I immediately applied what I learned to what I had recognized fell short in traditional self-help, motivation, and business books. I recognized that both philosophy and the virtues were the most powerful catalysts to increase personal performance and sustain success.

Things that were complex became simple and things that were fleeting became long-lasting, even permanent. By studying the Cardinal Virtues and applying them to my own life and the businesses I started and led, I began to understand things at a higher level. Unsurprisingly, I got results 10 times faster than ever before. Traditional motivational gurus taught simple techniques on how to make good decisions, one of these being the "Ben Franklin List" of positive versus negative reasons to do things. This is helpful, but the great minds I mentioned earlier taught the power of decision-making by mastering the virtue of Prudence. The Ben Franklin List approach is like an abacus; Prudence, the first Cardinal Virtue, is like a modern supercomputer.

There's a leadership deficit in the world today. That's not to say that there aren't many people in leadership roles. Rather, I'm saying there's a massive difference between a person filling a leadership role and a truly good leader. Put me onstage to sing opera, and I suppose you could call me an opera singer, but that doesn't make me a good vocalist. What we need are galvanized leaders, equipped with the strategies, tools, networks, and resources to enter into a new way of leadership and entrepreneurship. Yet this "new way" is in many ways very old. It's so old that it's new again, and it's simple and accessible. It can be most easily enacted by learning and living by the four Cardinal Virtues, of which I have already mentioned Prudence. Then, there are Justice, Fortitude, and Temperance. In this first section of *Leading Giants*, I'm going to outline each of these virtues as they can and should form the four cornerstones of not only your professional endeavors but your personal compass.

Living a virtuous life isn't pious or pretentious. It's practical and strategic. *Cardinal*, which is derived from *cardo*, is the Latin word for hinge, meaning all other virtues, like humility, compassion, and trustworthiness, hinge on how deeply you embody these four Cardinal Virtues. There are more than 60 virtues, but all fall short without the pursuit of the Cardinal Virtues. These four virtues build upon each other, meaning you can't have Fortitude or Justice until you develop Prudence. Just like you can't build a solid structure with only one cornerstone, you can't expect to succeed with only partial virtue. Thankfully, as you begin to become more virtuous, they all feed and inform the others.

Without further ado, let's begin!

Prudence: The Most Powerful Thing in the World Is a Decision

The measure of your success or failure will be determined by the decisions you make. Decisions are what set things in motion, and they have major impacts. They can make the world a better place or destroy it with the push of a button.

The power to love, hate, build up, or tear down others is only made possible through decisions. Therefore, virtues and vices imbue decision-making. If you want to build an organizational culture that's permeated by great decisions, then mastering the virtue of Prudence is your top priority. For Giants, it doesn't stop there. You also need to teach it to others. Prudence, the foundation of virtually every other virtue, is the gateway to building a great organization. Prudence is the first of what Aristotle called the Cardinal Virtues, which he believed and taught make a person happy and good, showing that they give someone the power to flourish.

Throughout history, Prudence was highly regarded and discussed. Now, when it is faintly mentioned, it's completely misrepresented. The word is more likely to be used to describe an uptight, sheepish, and even uncommitted person. It's also commonly used to describe a rigid person, called a "prude." Nothing could be further from the truth. If Prudence were a Marvel character, she would be ranked as the most powerful.

The Cardinal Virtues are crucial for building a great culture and for achieving long-term success. In fact, virtue is the greatest indicator for success, but it can't be measured by a Myers–Briggs test. If intelligence, experience, and skill were all equalized, who would be more successful? Would it be an honest, hardworking, fair person who makes good decisions or a lazy liar who makes bad decisions? The problem is that, for the most part, virtue and vice are hidden during job interviews and only come to life once a person begins their work. While intuition and experience can help identify the likelihood of a candidate being virtuous or filled with vice, it's difficult to know until you see them in action. The good news is that a great culture can shift a person on the continuum away from vice and toward virtue, which can make up for any deficits in character. We become like those we interact with, so a virtuous leader attracts virtuous followers, spreading virtue like a contagion to those willing to succeed.

By cultivating all four virtues within your organization, you eliminate complexities that other people unnecessarily add to their organizations. When the members of any group have higher levels of virtue, they'll make quicker decisions, creating efficiency. You have higher levels of trust, therefore less politics. You have better predictive analysis, therefore better business planning. The list goes on and on. That's why Prudence is the indisputable foundation of successful leadership and the necessary first step of this book. An added benefit to learning more about the Cardinal Virtues, as well as living them out, is that you will gain insights into human nature that will give you a distinct advantage as a leader. If applied wisely, you will attract and develop Giants because of it.

Words never said: "I loved working there because nobody could make a good decision."

TRUE STRENGTH COMES ONLY FROM VIRTUE

Oddly enough, I have had a select few people debate the idea that the virtues hold the merit that I promote. This is almost always predicated by a lack of understanding of the true nature of virtues. They fail to see that the Cardinal Virtues are like the muscles of your personal will and intellect. They can grow just as muscles can grow. They need a proper diet and exercise, and when provided, you'll become stronger than ever before. Having built all my companies with them at the forefront, I have experienced their value firsthand. The merits of virtue are best learned through personal experience, so I'd like to ask you a series of questions:

- Would you rather work with a good decision-maker or a poor one?
- Would you rather work with people who are efficient or so slow that you can't get anything done?
- Would you rather work with arrogant, prideful people or humble, team-oriented people?
- Would you rather work with fair people or cheaters?
- Would you rather work with courageous people or cowards?
- Would you rather work with lazy people or hardworking people?

Fundamentally, each of these options exemplifies working with a virtuous person or a vice-oriented person. Any vice within an individual will impact an organizational culture, like cracks in the foundation. If not prevented, the waters of vice will cause cracks, seep in, and erode what you're building. The reason I focus on the virtues rather than traditional motivational terms like grit or tenacity is because the mastery of Prudence, for example, contains within it many sub-virtues. Motivational moods are whimsical, as I wrote about extensively in my book *Perpetual Motivation*, but virtue goes far beyond just behaving a particular way on any given day.[1]

The effect of being virtuous is that you actually become someone new with better results because virtues are habits that you work to embody rather than catchy ideas you get in a corporate training that you try out for a while.

When someone speaks of high-minded ideas like Prudence, it may be difficult for some people to get excited. Even if you find the topic compelling, you might think, *Well, that's nice, Dave, but how do I get Prudence?* As a young man, I was frustrated by advice I knew was good, but that I didn't know how to apply, such as, "You've got to believe to achieve." That sounded fine and all, but I still didn't know how to go from not believing to believing. "I believe I can fly" might have been enough for Peter Pan, but for me, I needed solid, actionable advice. Thankfully, there is a way to instill belief, and I will get to that in future works. For now, let's get into the nitty-gritty about how to master Prudence and know how to make great decisions. In no time, you'll realize how practical it is to obtain and teach.

There are three areas of focus when working to master Prudence:

- The first three steps to a great decision
- The importance of secondary decisions
- What gets in the way of good decisions

THE FIRST THREE STEPS

Aristotle defined Prudence in his *Nicomachean Ethics* as "a state grasping the truth, involving reason, concerned with action about things that are good or bad for a human being."[2] This basically means that a prudential person comes to the knowledge of the right thing to do in a given situation and then acts on it. While I highly encourage you to read deeper works on Prudence, I will make this less philosophical and more practical. The first three steps to mastering a decision are:

1. **Counsel:** Conceiving the best outcome and the best way to attain it. I call this **desiring what is good** (about the given situation).
2. **Judgment:** Choosing the most effective means for attaining the end. For simplicity's sake, I will refer to this as **knowing what is real**.
3. **Command:** The action of carrying out the deed. I will call this **doing what is good**. (Note: My titles in bold are influenced by Josef Pieper's book *The Four Cardinal Virtues*.)[3]

Think about any situation in life. If you don't take this first step to Prudence, of **desiring what is good**, then how can you have a positive outcome in anything—i.e., make a good decision? If you don't desire what is good in a relationship, how can you make good decisions that cultivate love and respect? If your Uber driver doesn't desire what is good, do you want him behind the wheel? If your surgeon doesn't desire what is good, do you want him operating on you? If your boss doesn't desire what is good, would you trust her to lead you? Or, if you are the boss, and your employees don't desire what is good, would you delegate to them? Of course not. Desiring what is good is the first and most basic step toward mastering Prudence.

Goodness is more than just one element of the decision. If a married person desires someone other than his or her spouse, there is no good outcome unless a decision is made to abandon the target of the desire altogether. If an employee desires to falsely portray their productivity, there is no good outcome for themselves or their employer other than doing the work. So, in addition to the choice to be and do good, the circumstance itself must also be good. Desiring what is good also means being "considerate" about things versus being rash, which is a vice counter to Prudence. You must consider things to avoid rashness. For example, if an employee walks into your office while you're on your computer and asks you a question that you barely grasped because your mind was someplace else and you answer without considering the question or the ramifications of the answer, you might rashly give an approval to a bad idea. So . . . "consider it" before you answer.

In business, this is how Prudence works. Let's say you're a baker, and your specialty is gourmet cookies. What is good in this given situation? Baking delicious and artful cookies at a fair price. There are other good things that can be desired, but that's a sufficient summary. If you don't desire those basic good things, then you can't hope to obtain them. Even worse, if you desire overpriced, ugly, and disgusting cookies, then you're out of business before you start. Your business partners, investors, and eventually your customers will provide the counsel you need to conceive of the best cookies you can possibly make, providing what you need to bring this goodness to market.

In order to make these good cookies, you need to make judgments or **know what is real**. Let's say you experiment with some new recipes and serve them to a room of 20 willing volunteers. You ask, "What do you think of the cookies?" to which the universal reply is, "They taste horrible!"

If you fail to accept the feedback and instead respond by saying, "You're tasting them wrong!" you're living outside of reality. As silly as that might sound, many people would rather be "right" to their own demise than be "wrong" and gain prosperity, a concept you'll see again in chapter 16.

The main vices that work against **knowing what is real** are precipitation and negligence. Precipitation is the failure to accept good advice and/or acting too quickly. Negligent people either ignore good advice or never seek it before taking action. To **know what is real**, you must consider the counsel of others or facts of a given circumstance. In this metaphor, it would be to listen to the volunteers. Failing to do so guarantees overall failure. So, as you ask more questions, you may get universal feedback that the cookies are too dry, not sweet enough, etc. This allows you to identify the best approach to make delicious cookies.

So, what's left in knowing how to make great decisions? The third step is command, or **doing what is good**. A prudent person not only desires what is good and knows what is real, he or she acts on what they know. So, back to the analogy, by **doing what is good**, the baker revises the recipe, gets great feedback, and sells tons of cookies. This is good, not only for business but also for providing others with a quality product having gone through the necessary steps to succeed.

When people fail to act on what is good, you see other vices counter to Prudence manifest, such as inconsistency or slowness. An imprudent person is notoriously inconsistent. So, if you work with an inconsistent person, train them in these three steps of counsel, judgment, and command. Likewise, many people take action but not based on what is real. They manipulate data or try to push an idea along just because it was theirs. Driven by ego, they ignore good counsel yet move forward. They possess additional vices counter to Prudence such as craftiness, deceit, and fraud. So, if you want honest, hardworking, and good decision-makers, train them first and foremost on Prudence. This is the essential foundation that must be mastered to be a Leader of Giants.

The example of cookies risks being such a simplified one that you might not receive it for its true weight. That would be a mistake. This tiny little formula of **desiring what is good**, **knowing what is real**, and **doing what is good** is like a snowball at the top of a mountain. I recommend applying this formula to personal past examples of well-made decisions as well as poor decisions. Humble self-discovery is a great way to understand not only yourself but the overall human nature of all those you lead. Humble leaders have the advantage of recognizing general human temptations in themselves; therefore, they learn to make better judgments about the people they lead.

So, begin with yourself—you alone hold the ability to change your own actions and, in time, influence the actions of those you lead. Then, analyze what may have been behind the behaviors of others on the team. Be careful here, though. The purpose of this analysis is to gain intuition, which is supported by personal experience, but not to believe that you can know the true motives of others. Being a humble leader means you will first ask questions with a curious and empathetic point of view, adding context to your intuition or changing your perspective.

This exercise allows you to understand patterns that ordinary people have so you can inspire unbeatable behaviors that create extraordinary success.

EXAMPLE DECISION: "HOW DO WE ENTER A NEW MARKET?"

Did I desire what is good? Did I go to that meeting to make sure people liked my idea to bolster my ego or did I go because I wanted to find the best idea for the business? In other words, did I desire what was good for the organization or did I put myself first?

Did I know what is real? Was my ego bruised because my rival colleague's idea was accepted and not mine? Did I debate during the meeting based on what made me feel respected or based on what the best idea was for the business?

Did I do what is good? Did I cast my final vote to bolster my self-esteem or based on what was best for the team?

It fascinates me that many executives skip this sort of analysis within their organizations and in their own lives. Often, leaders miss the motive behind how and why people make decisions. They fixate on data alone versus the way human nature intermingles with data. This is often the difference between a naive leader and a leader who thinks dynamically, operating like an organizational alchemist who sees the way the varied ingredients of a circumstance influence the outcome.

THE IMPORTANCE OF SECONDARY DECISIONS

You are reading this book because you made a decision, and that decision was preceded by others, like buying the book or receiving it as a gift. Your primary decision was to buy it and secondary was to read it, which you're doing now. Then, as you continue reading, you'll be given countless opportunities to make more secondary decisions such as to apply or not apply the insights within. With that in mind, I have witnessed many people make big primary decisions but not solid secondary decisions, which are necessary to bring primary decisions to fulfillment. They may decide to get a job but not to be great at it. They may decide to take a foreign language class but, ironically, not to practice in order to learn the language. They may decide to have a child but not to be a great parent, or to get married but not to have a great marriage. There are always additional decisions that must be made to fortify the pursuit of what was initially decided.

How often have you been invited to a meeting only to have no good come from it? Or how often have you been in a meeting where great ideas abound, but nothing happens with them after the fact? It is crucial to set out the vision for secondary decisions that need to be made based on the primary or initial decision. This is classically called "thinking it through." If you decide to do XYZ, what responsibilities will ensue? What decisions will you need to make for the primary decision to be worth it?

It's an art form to psycho-navigate an "if/then" situation. In other words, you're wise to theorize about the secondary decisions before you even make the primary decision. This allows you to understand the level of commitment you are entering with the primary decision, following through with your word and deed. Do this and you'll be a superhero no matter where you work. Remember, if Prudence were a Marvel character, she'd be right at the top. And so will you.

WHAT GETS IN THE WAY OF MAKING GOOD DECISIONS

It is important to consider some of the things that can hinder good decision-making. At the top of the list is ego. When we make decisions to satisfy our self-esteem, we become irrational. If you have ever worked with or been in a relationship with someone who has narcissistic tendencies, you know what I mean. You find yourself saying, "Wait, what? That doesn't make sense." "Why did they react that way?" "How do they see it that way?" "What made them so upset?" Someone with these behaviors causes confusion, creates division, and destroys a healthy culture.

Those who don't suffer from a diagnosed mental disorder can also make harmful choices driven by ego. Consider a scenario involving two coworkers, Joe and Ally. Joe had recently expressed personal interest in Ally, which she politely declined. Some weeks later in a team meeting, Ally voiced her opinion about a particular project strategy. Even though her approach had merit, Joe, still stinging from the rejection, immediately opposed it without any sound rationale. To an outsider, Joe's disagreement might seem based on professional differences, but a closer look would reveal it as a decision fueled by wounded ego rather than objective analysis. When our egos are bruised or wanton, we act nothing less than crazy at times. So, put your ego aside or stand on the sidelines until it's in check before making important decisions.

Second, our emotions can get in the way. Unbridled passion would also go under this umbrella. (No need to take time telling you why decisions under that banner can go wrong!) Emotions are occasionally driven by ego, so there is some overlap, but even positive emotions can negatively impact our ability to make good decisions. A good example is when people experience happy moods, they often become more lax in their standards. However, I want to point out that emotions need not be in competition with our decision-making. When our emotions are aligned with the desire for what is good as well as the reality of the situation, they can fuel us when we respond, command, or act. When we do what is good, we excel. The key is to make sure your intellect leads your emotions. Feel your emotions, but always maintain a slight edge of clear reasoning. Make your decisions with calm judgment and a focus on **knowing what is real**.

The third major hindrance to decision-making is a lack of information. This one is perplexing to me based on how common it is. I have been in way too many meetings where I witnessed people make decisions without enough information. Taking action without a reasonable dose of information is classically imprudent. So then, what is a reasonable dose? It's the amount of information needed to assess the upside and downside of a situation or opportunity before the time passes to act. For example, if a nurse asks a doctor, "Should we give the patient the medicine?" is there any other choice? Will they die without it? Will they die because of it? How long do they have before it's critically needed? These are important questions to ask and they demonstrate that, on one hand, perpetual discernment is not possible, and on the other hand, rash decisions are potentially harmful. Cultivate a studious culture by encouraging lots of questions. Show your team that you are willing to question your own ideas and, if need be, abandon them for a better one when alternate information presents itself.

> *Measuring the speed of your decisions against the weight of the issue is a good rule of thumb.*

Finally, the fourth major hindrance for good decision-making is bias. Bias is not the same as bad intentions, although they can resemble each other. Bad intentions are nonstarters for good decision-making because a good decision always includes **desiring what is good**. A person can be earnest about desiring what is good, but bias muddies the water. Let's say you want to add a new product to your mix, and you come from a particular industry that you left because you failed. It is likely that, while you desire what is best for the company, your negative bias toward the old product may get in the way of your decision-making. You may confuse the actual product with a poor marketing strategy or a poorly executed plan. If you are able to put your bias aside, you can add tremendous value to the discussion because you can see that the product idea may be good but you are now able to provide executional cautions to bolster success.

These insights serve as a mirror, reflecting not just your own motivations but also the undercurrents driving your team's behaviors. Before jumping into decisions, take a moment to introspect and gauge the deeper motivations at play. Applying Prudence is key to your success. By doing so, you'll be well on your way to reaching Giant status.

GIANT TAKEAWAYS

The effect of being virtuous is that you actually become someone new with better results, because virtues are habits that you work to embody rather than catchy ideas you get in a corporate training and then try out for a while. And so, because Prudence is the foundational virtue, the measure of your success or failure will be determined by the decisions you make.

Here is how to become prudent:

- Implement the three steps of great decision-making.
  1. **Counsel:** Desire what is good.
  2. **Judgment:** Know what is real.
  3. **Command:** Do what is good.
- Prioritize the importance of secondary decisions.
- Don't let these things get in the way of good decisions: ego, emotions not balanced with desiring/knowing/doing what is good, a lack of information, and bias.

2

Justice: A Moral Quality or Habit That Perfects the Will and Inclines It to Render to Each and All What Belongs to Them

When it comes down to it, most people who leave organizations under negative circumstances usually find something or someone to be "unfair." If they say, "The culture was bad," they tag on, "and that wasn't fair." "I was overlooked for a promotion, and that wasn't fair." "They never listened to my ideas, which was unfair." No matter what the specific reason, fairness is usually the summary point. On the other hand, people stay and are happy when they think things are fair. You can sum up most exit interviews two ways: "They treated me fairly and I liked it," or "They treated me unfairly and I didn't like it." So, who decides what is fair? After all, most people consider themselves to be just.

The virtue of Justice is simply defined but can be complex in application. The shortest definition for Justice is "the firm will to give someone

25

their due." In other words, it's to give people what they have a moral right to have. This includes judicial punishments for a committed crime or compensation won in a civil case. Justice is the fair and impartial treatment of all, ensuring rights are upheld and wrongs are redressed. It's the foundation of societal and cultural harmony, preventing chaos by ensuring fairness.

So, how does this apply to leadership? Classically, there are three directions that Justice flows in society and those three directions are represented in the microcosm of any organizational culture. They are inspired by the classical understanding of Justice and how it flows in society. Leaders must ensure the environment and culture allow for these to happen:

- **Communitive Justice:** This is the Justice that exists between employees and coworkers. This includes the exchange of services they provide to each other.
- **Organization to Employee Justice:** This includes having a right to a good culture that includes respect and access to the tools, resources, and authority they need to get their job done effectively. This type of Justice also applies from the organization to the customer (Descending Vertical). Fair compensation to employees for the work they do applies here.
- **Employee to Organization Justice (Ascending Vertical):** This is where, among other things, the employees owe the organization good participation in the culture and an honest day's work.

Before diving into the flow of Justice, I will remind you that you can't have Justice without Prudence. Therefore, unsurprisingly, there are three things that inhibit Justice, and they all result from leaders lacking Prudence. I will come back to these three points throughout the chapter:

1. A lack of desire for what is good
2. Not knowing what is real
3. Not pursuing what is good

26

COMMUNITIVE JUSTICE

To understand how Justice works within leadership, I will be using several familial and social examples. While seemingly unrelated, they provide solid insights into the way all humans interact (human nature, which never changes) and draw out a good reflection on organizational Justice. Many years ago, a close friend of mine went through a divorce. I was awkwardly and circumstantially present during an argument between him and his soon-to-be ex-wife. Both were very close to their two children, and the kids loved and respected each parent equally. So, the major point of pain for all involved was deciding on how many days the kids would spend with either parent. If I had not heard this for myself, I wouldn't have believed it, but she said, "We can divide the kids between us totally evenly, right down the center. I get them 75% of the time and you get them 25% of the time." Not only was that bad math, but it was not fair for the kids or their father. I bring this up because, although it is not an organizational example, it is similar to the types of injustices felt in organizations. His future ex-wife was uninterested in what was good and what was real. Therefore, Justice could not take place in the communitive sense and the kids paid the highest price. When employees fail in the same sense, other employees suffer, and so do clients and customers even if it is delayed or indirect. Giants consider the impact that small and large injustices have on the rest of the organization all the way to the end user of the products or services.

When people who have no sense of Justice are in positions of power, terrible things happen.

Throughout world history we have seen radical views of Justice that run counter to human nature and would never work in a practical sense.

For example, socialism and communism fail 100% of the time because they run against human nature and Justice. Applying socialist standards to the workplace would make it collapse virtually overnight. Of course, socialists will argue against that point saying that I have no understanding of either leadership or socialism. I know this because they have commented this way on my YouTube channel; however, it is easy to dismiss the views of people who ignore a 100-year, hard-core, irrefutable historical reality (second step to Prudence). But I'm writing this book for leaders, not socialists, so the point is moot.

Nobody in their right mind would open a sales meeting by saying, "Linda and Omar, fantastic job selling five times more than Eric, Antwon, and Annie who took off last week to go to the beach. To be fair to them, I will give them half of your commissions since you have earned more than they did." That would be the last day you see Linda and Omar, and it would be the beginning of Eric, Antwon, and Annie demanding even more for less effort, ultimately leading to you going out of business.

There is an interesting blend of application between all three flows of Justice. Compensation is one of those unique circumstances in which Justice flows in all directions. If a manager agrees to pay an employee a certain compensation, then it is now due to the employee (descending). However, the employee must then do the work (ascending), and both the employee and the manager need to honor the spirit of the agreement (communitive). Each of these is bolstered by human nature and the way we interact with incentives. Anyone who has raised children knows that if you clean their room for them, they won't learn to do it on their own. Why? Human beings naturally do whatever they please when there is no perceived consequence to their bad behavior, like a child who gets the reward of enjoying the comforts of a clean room without putting forth any effort to clean it. It's hard to blame a child or anyone else for enjoying benefits without effort. To a degree, it's somewhat complimentary to the child's intellect. Why work when you get the reward anyway? However, it is not a compliment to their virtue or development. Laziness makes life unlivable, personally, communally, and culturally. There's no Justice when you participate in the retardation of a person by rewarding them for something unmerited.

ORGANIZATION TO EMPLOYEE JUSTICE (DESCENDING VERTICAL)

If you give someone something for nothing,
they will want even more for less.

The virtue of Justice is interesting. There is a clearly personal, individual aspect, meaning that the individual leader must develop the virtue of Justice to lead as a Giant, but Justice extends beyond his or her own virtue into the organization. The "collective" idea of virtue is found in this descending vertical from the organization to the member or employee and to the clients or customers. It is summarized or felt in the culture of the organization, which is why I will spend most of my time on this aspect of Justice. It's also discovered within policies, which, to a degree, act like laws within an organization. The first policy I implement when I found a company is **we don't believe in policy for policy's sake**. You know what it's like to be tortured by a nonthinking customer service agent who puts you into a policy category that has nothing to do with your situation. It immediately triggers your sense of Justice. Consider a no-returns policy that incudes no money back after purchases. Well, if the product never arrived to the client because the company failed to deliver it, the "no refunds" policy misses the point by not considering the full situation. So, the strongest way to have Justice for clients is to look at whether the policy makes sense in each particular case.

When employees say "the culture was toxic," they are speaking of the essence of the organization and fairness, or collective Justice. When the leader exhibits personal virtues, they are often emulated but that's not automatic and it can't happen by dictate. Those behaviors are either accepted and cultivated by other team members or rejected. The leader then needs to correct, prune, and weed out behaviors counter to the virtue of Justice or they will exist despite his or her personal application of it directly. This is where his or her extended influence is felt. The number of ways it is felt is limitless.

This is most readily seen when you give someone something for nothing; they will want even more for less. This attitude will permeate a culture and throw off each flow of Justice. Many people will go from expecting something for nothing, to acting poorly (which is worse than doing nothing), and then wanting a reward for their newly adopted bad behavior. They will even say, "I deserve it!" They act this way because they fail to apply the second step to Prudence: knowing what is real. And when it becomes a pervasive part of a culture, there becomes a collective injustice.

On the opposite side of the spectrum, I have witnessed leaders take advantage of people by paying them too little or working them too hard. That behavior makes the owner or boss act entitled by assuming they deserve something (hard work) for nothing or little (low pay or no pay for overtime). This again is a failure to know what is real and creates injustice both communitively and in the descending fashion. As long as the vices of greed, power, laziness, and entitlement exist in you or in the culture of your organization, you will not experience the peace, prosperity, or productivity that is available to you. The same is true for your personal life; the virtue of Justice is directly related to influence and power. People want to follow fair people because they trust and feel protected by them. The trust that comes from Justice creates efficiency within your organization. Low trust slows things down by creating hesitancy. Stephen M. R. Covey wrote a book aptly called *The Speed of Trust*. It's a rare book because the title summarizes the entire point of the text in four words.

Trust can be broken in many ways but there is a subtle way that many people disregard. Imagine challenging someone to run a race on a pebble-filled parking lot and then taking their shoes away before you begin. Your opponent would claim it isn't fair, and they'd be right. That stands as a metaphor for when employers ask team members to manage roles and responsibilities but fail to provide them the authority, tools, and resources to get the job done. This breaks trust because it creates doubt in the mind of the employee. They doubt the leaders grasp the fullness of the challenge (aka they don't know reality) or think they are being set up to fail. When this happens, especially as a pattern, it erodes culture and is unfair. Be sure to provide the authority, tools, and resources for employees to do what is asked of them.

Descending Justice Has Nuance, Which Is Often Counterintuitive

Justice is not always as linear as most would like it to be. Mitigating circumstances, one-off situations, and limited information require leaders to make specialized decisions outside the norm. Building the virtue of Justice allows for leaders to use their knowledge of human nature and intuition to make judgments. King Solomon, known biblically as the wisest man to have lived, used his understanding of human nature and intuition to make judicial decisions in his court. Famously, he mediated an argument between two women who both claimed to be the mother of the same baby. His solution, knowing it would never happen, was to cut the baby in half so they could both have him. He knew that the true mother would plead for the life of the child by offering that the impostor take the child. His plan worked and he was able to give the healthy child to the true mother and Justice was served.

Leaders have a distinct advantage when they study human nature and make decisions considering it. Only through the virtue of Justice can you make fair decisions about compensation, sales negotiating, and, truly, every other aspect of leadership. At times, Justice is counterintuitive. For example, let's say you have an employee who tried his best to earn a bonus but fell short. You like him and see that he has a promising future. His performance wasn't quite enough to capture the bonus, despite earnest efforts. You're aware that he really needs the bonus to meet a difficult family need. If he doesn't get the bonus, he's likely to look for a new job with more pay, and you know his resume is strong enough for him to do so. You also know that if he got his bonus, he'd stay.

How do you justify paying him his bonus to retain him if he missed earning it? Should you even attempt to pay it? If you do pay it, is it fair to others who also didn't reach their goal? These are good questions. Some leaders just say, "He missed it, too bad." At times this is the right move, but if this talented person moves on, what's the cost of replacing him? Or if you do pay it and the others who earned it find out, can you justify that to them?

A creative and just solution, which admittedly may not apply to all situations but is worth exploring, would be to find a new way for him to get enough money to stay. If you simply pay the old bonus, you reward low performance and create injustice for those who also didn't earn it. Not to mention there is an injustice to those who did the work, earning it through merit. If you ignore his needs and his earnest effort, you risk losing him and reducing his morale. A just leader could say, "Sorry, Joe, you missed the bonus." That is a just conclusion, but here's something most people miss about Justice: it is tied intimately to mercy.

Justice without mercy is cold and inconsiderate. High-level leaders are thoughtful, so they consider mitigating circumstances and exercise their authority in a nuanced way. A Giant would try something like this: "Joe, you have worked diligently to achieve your goals and to hit your bonus. You're well on your way to being a top performer, but I think I gave you too much ground to cover. Had you been lazy or negligent, I would not be doing what I am about to do. But your work ethic and the way you fit the culture have merited a chance to get a new bonus in a relatively short time so that your financial needs can be met. Here's the plan . . ." By setting up a new target that can be met, he will be relieved, appreciative, and now, fiercely loyal. There are obviously things to consider here, such as how you may include all the team members who missed the bonus and possibly provide a new incentive to the people who did earn it. The point remains: thinking artfully is important.

Justice is not simply something that we distribute; it's something we perceive, feel, and want. In many cases, when people are invited to partake in an entitlement, they reject the idea because it "doesn't feel right." Their sense of Justice prevents others from giving them something for nothing. To be fair, there is Justice in making sure those who can't help themselves are helped. Providing for people who are legitimately struggling is part of Justice and an obligation we should all consider.

The following example is basic, so to some degree, you may know "how" to handle this, but it illustrates where trust and injustice may be perceived. My point in sharing is the "why," not the how. When you know the "why," you can be more effective in the "how." Let's say you offer someone a job for $100K per year and they counter with $130K, to which you immediately respond, "Okay." By doing so, you've put doubt in their mind, which was triggered by a sense of Justice. *Why didn't he offer that to start with? Is he taking advantage of me? Should I have said $150K?* You can prevent the doubt by responding with, "We can do $130K if you can start a month earlier"—or anything of value in exchange for more pay. Exchanging the higher comp with a new start date offsets the alarm in their head that screams "injustice." I've found that it really doesn't matter what the exchange of value is as long as it is something reasonable. This prevents the "something for nothing" effect that triggers injustice.

Oftentimes, an inexperienced salesperson presents a price only to have the prospective customer balk at it. The knee-jerk reaction for an inexperienced sales rep is to immediately reduce the price. So, let's say you offer a product for sale priced at $2K. The prospect asks, "How about $1,500?" If you simply say, "Okay," then you have a problem. You put doubt in the customer's mind. It can suggest desperation, which can come off as insecurity about the product. It can also make it appear that others may not be interested in the product, therefore creating an anti-mimetic desire. *Why did he reduce the price so easily? Is something wrong with the product? Am I being taken advantage of?* It's a wise practice to only reduce price in exchange for something such as buying now, extending the length or duration of the contract, or trading out a feature. In almost all cases, this can satisfy the need for a more satisfactory price without triggering their sense of Justice.

Over decades of tracking this sort of thing, I have noticed that clients in various types of businesses who receive the biggest discounts without anything in exchange are the most difficult to satisfy long term. They also have lower renewal rates than those who "earned" a discount by signing on-the-spot or committing to a longer-term relationship. This all stems from strained trust due to their innate sense of Justice, albeit a reverse application of Justice, which is self-inflicted in these examples.

EMPLOYEE TO ORGANIZATION JUSTICE (ASCENDING VERTICAL)

This is a topic that primarily relates to the way employees and team members are required to serve Justice to the organization. This comes primarily by doing an honest day's work and honoring the spirit of their agreements or contracts. It is a fuller topic for a book on how to be an irreplaceable team member, but I would be remiss to diminish it as it relates to leaders. For a leader to be just, they must determine when the culture, policies, or employees in their organization are being unjust toward each other, but they also need to determine if employees are acting justly toward the organization. Building an organization that makes the spirit of the agreement between parties known is important. Defining what is expected and providing examples of what it means to honor those results versus fall short is important. Set clear expectations of outcomes and activities whenever possible. If those standards are clear and the employees are empowered to get them done but they fail, look at the possibility of them not owning their end of the relationship.

Young People Today!

The greatest challenge when it comes to Ascending Vertical Justice is that it relies on the virtue of others, which makes it less controllable. Inconsistent virtues show up most often with entry-level employees who tend to be younger. This is because there is less time to recognize good versus bad behaviors in newer, less experienced people compared to more advanced employees who have already proven themselves. Assuming that younger people have the same level of virtue as older generations will lead to great frustration. Most often, virtue is developed over time, so older people often have higher levels. Still every generation seems to complain about the coming generation being less virtuous than the previous. Because of that, I mostly dismiss generational complaints in both directions. In fact, an article in the *Harvard Business Review* supports my hesitation. The article basically says that many studies show that the perceptions we have about younger generations are not substantiated with data.[1]

Despite being skeptical about huge generational differences in some ways, in others I am aware that there are some very real, fast-moving societal and technological changes that cause certain shifts in younger employees. This impacts the way they process things when they enter the workplace. These statistics are wildly different than previous generations. My observations are not made as a judgment. I bring them to your attention clinically so you can consider ways to effectively motivate, influence, and communicate with your teams.

- The majority of kids today are not raised in a household with both married biological parents.
- Fatherlessness is paramount.
- Families are having fewer children; therefore, sibling dynamics have changed.

These three statistical realities create a unique circumstance for organizations. There are other factors to consider but, for the most part, the other factors are the ones that end up being more about generational biases and are not grounded in evidence as the aforementioned *HBR* article addresses. The family has always been considered the cell of society where children learn virtues and develop resilience against vice. Lest anyone take what I'm saying as a judgment, I have been through divorce. As a result, I am fully aware of the challenges children face when they are not in the same home as their biological mother and father, full-time. It is important to look past whatever your personal situation is and to look at the situation dispassionately, as a leader.

Children who have gone through their parents' divorce inherently have greater challenges than those who have not. A sensitive topic, I realize, but I want to offer statistics that elucidate this often-painful reality because it is relevant to how you must lead. Armed with this knowledge, you can prevent or diminish the negative impacts.

- **Divorce and Academic Achievement:** Children of divorced parents are twice as likely to drop out of high school than their peers who are still living with parents who did not divorce.[2]

- **Divorce and Behavioral Issues:** Children of divorce are at a greater risk to experience injury, asthma, headaches, and speech defects than children whose parents have not divorced.[3]
- **Divorce and Psychological Effects:** Teenagers in single-parent families and in blended families are 300% more likely to need psychological help within any given year than teens from intact, nuclear families.[4]
- **Fatherless Homes and Crime:** 85% of all children who show behavior disorders come from fatherless homes—20 times the average.[5]
- **Fatherless Homes and Drug Abuse:** Children from fatherless homes are more likely to abuse drugs and alcohol.[6]
- **Fatherless Homes and Suicide:** Children of single-parent households are more likely to commit suicide.[7]
- **Fatherless Homes and Imprisonment:** 70% of juveniles in state-operated institutions come from fatherless homes.[8]
- **Divorce and Teen Pregnancy:** Teen girls who live with single mothers are more likely to get pregnant than those who live with both parents.[9]

It's essential to interpret these statistics with caution. They show correlation, not causation. Many factors, including economic hardship, the quality of parenting post-divorce, the parents' mental health, community resources, and religious upbringing (or lack thereof) can influence people's outcomes. Despite the challenges, many children of divorced parents are fully able to grow up to be successful, happy, and well-adjusted adults. This is not about success or failure. It's about the way they see Justice and injustice, especially at work.

Perceptions of Justice are radically altered when a person loses their sense of security via family dynamics. While this book is not about this from a social perspective, it is about insights that can help you lead people who have been through this common struggle in an empathetic way. Here's how you can look at it: If your parents don't teach you Justice (or any other virtue), then relatives and neighbors step in. However, families are more scattered, and people don't know their neighbors as well. So, teachers or coaches must do their best to influence kids. This is inherently more difficult without parental support, so it fails more often than not. If teachers and coaches fail, then who's left? A mentor or a boss is usually next in line. It's not that young people aren't taught anything outside of a traditional home environment; it's that even the good lessons by great parents are weakened and diluted. Simply put, if a parent is there only half the time, he or she has half the time to educate and influence. This is why many young adults are "half-ready" for life. It's partially why they have half a work ethic or half a sense of right or wrong, oftentimes acting like a 15-year-old in a 30-year-old body.

In a strangely related way, it's why the military recently released that one of the greatest challenges it faces is recruiting "skinny-fat" people:

"And one problem the Army faces these days," according to Friedl, a specialist in physiological performance, "is a high number of 'skinny-fat' recruits. These people don't look out of shape but, indeed, are because of sedentary lifestyles that have left them with low muscle mass and frail bones and connective tissue. At Ft. Moore in Georgia, new soldiers are given calcium supplements to counter a recent uptick in broken feet and bones in the legs, according to several senior soldiers in charge of training. It's guys who look good in skinny jeans, but they have high fat because there's no muscle," Friedl said.[10]

The soft lifestyle of many young people is not only a physical problem; it's a problem of resolve. Resolve goes hand in hand with the virtue of Fortitude. As I highlighted in chapter 1, the Cardinal Virtues are interconnected. You can't fully possess Justice without Prudence, nor can you have true Fortitude without Justice. Thus, someone lacking resolve likely struggles with fairness as well. This connection often goes unnoticed by those deficient in the Cardinal Virtues.

Another way the Cardinal Virtues are connected includes the over- or under-reaction to situations, which is almost always identified under the virtue of Justice. This is why it's so important for young people to learn to regulate Justice as early as possible in life. For example, in an attempt to correct discrimination, which should be done, some people go so far as to create reverse discrimination, which is just as bad. This behavior creates either a hypocritical environment and destroys culture or an ignorant, weak environment, which also destroys culture.

The most significant takeaway you should gather from the statistics and commentary I just shared is this: be patient with younger people when it comes to issues of Justice because the younger generations operate at a very high emotional level on this issue, which prevents them from making fair judgments. In a nutshell, if you patiently and intellectually explain the way Justice works and live it out so they can feel it, they will see the beauty in it, the truth behind it, and the feeling of unity it creates.

MISGUIDED APPLICATIONS OF JUSTICE ABOUND

"If I did it for you, I'd need to do it for everyone," is not Justice.

Imagine Keith, who has been an excellent performer and is committed to your company. Tragically, he comes on hard times with a sick child. Needing flexibility, he asks to come in later two days a week to take his child to treatment. He's still willing to get the full job done, but he just needs some flexibility. His team lead says, "If I did that for you, I'd have to do it for everyone." This often-misguided concept of Justice can be ineffective and unfair. Its misapplication in a case like this causes Keith to immediately find a new and more flexible job. Because Keith was treated without empathy, his coworkers Ellen and Marcus felt the proverbial straw that broke the camel's back and used the situation as motivation to finally leave too. So, the team lead now needs to replace three good people while the employees who are morally weak or aloof and saw nothing wrong with his decision remain. These are the strange, subtle situations that transform organizations into low morale work environments.

In addition to this example, I must say the following is so elementary that when I was a young man, had I read this by another author, I would have found it bizarre that they'd need to include it. But over the years, I have learned not to be shocked by the shortcomings of adult professionals, so these simple examples are necessary, and I am compelled to include them.

There have been times when I have rewarded top performers beyond our agreed-upon compensation. Sometimes, I did so with perks, other times financially. In either case, I remember once being told by a lesser-performing team member that what I did was not fair because he didn't get the same treatment. I quickly responded, "No, I've treated you and will treat you just as fair. You have my promise that when you break the sales record like she did, I will give you the same reward." His reaction was swift and sincere. He immediately agreed that it was the fair way to handle it. So, despite his knee-jerk "not fair" emotional reaction, he saw the Justice once the elementary reasoning was explained. The striking thing was how he, due to his emotions, simply didn't consider the reward/merit relationship even though he earned commission. It was a profound thought to him, almost to an embarrassing, self-admitting degree. He was in an "everyone gets a trophy" paradigm as a full-grown man.

GREAT PEOPLE ARE EVERYWHERE

*It's unjust to put a person
in a role they can't handle.*

While I prefer to use data to support a point, the following short point is merely my personal observation over 35 years and should be read with that in mind. It is, however, formed not only in light of my observations but logically supported by the statistical changes in family dynamics, advances in technology, and how they impact the recruiting pool. My observation is that one-third of the recruits are unable to work effectively, meaning they don't grasp or have the capacity to fulfill the responsibilities asked of them. This is a much larger number than when I began my career. Despite many of them having advanced degrees, being intelligent, and using technology effectively, they struggle to understand the fundamental nature of reality, knowledge, and existence. This, along with rapid changes in technology, has created a softness of character due to lifestyle.

Another one-third are brilliant and hardworking. In fact, I'd say this group is more brilliant and harder working than in any other time. The main difference between these two groups is that the former has been told what to think, leading to their demise. Therefore, they are unable to solve problems on their own. They are unable to face difficulties without someone running to their aid while they scream victim. They have no tolerance for anyone who does not agree with them, and they only accept people who shower them with unending affirmation. When the affirmations aren't enough, they turn on those who don't soothe their egos. The problem is that the real world is not like that, nor should it ever become like that. The latter one-third has been taught how to think effectively. Therefore, they are able to deduce right from wrong, ugly from beautiful, and truth from a lie. They are able to problem-solve, and they can endure disagreement and thoughts not consistent with their own beliefs. They are tough and they have a sense of Justice. However, not all of them have been given training on how to apply their intellect to a noble cause.

Thankfully, the last one-third is a group who are in between. They can be influenced and educated. They have grasped natural law and right reason such that the silly cultural ideas, which inevitably fail and make no sense, don't erode their keen eye, open mind, and good-natured heart. Likely, those who do entertain certain harmful contemporary notions have simply not been shown good alternative ideals. This is why when they hear about the Cardinal Virtues and the Transcendentals—the universal desires such as unity, beauty, truth, and goodness, which we'll discuss in chapter 5—they light up with enthusiasm. They can grow rapidly into very effective team members, but you need to teach them how. They're budding Giants wanting to be led, and who better to lead them than someone committed to taking ordinary people to extraordinary levels of success.

GIANT TAKEAWAYS

Justice is the fair and impartial treatment of all, ensuring rights are upheld and wrongs are redressed. It's the foundation of societal, cultural, and organizational harmony, preventing chaos by ensuring fairness. Like a judge has a gavel, here are some tools to enact Justice:

- **Fairness:** Perceptions of fairness greatly influence employee satisfaction and retention, so strive for transparent and equitable treatment of all people, all the time.

- **Empathic Decision-Making:** Justice is intimately tied to mercy. Making fair decisions that factor in empathy always leads to better long-term outcomes for both the organization and the individuals involved.

- **Nuanced Thinking:** Most situations that require Justice have mitigating or specific details that need to be taken into consideration. Ignoring those details is lazy. Giants do the mental work required to be fair.

- **Reward Accountability, Crush Entitlement:** Avoid creating a sense of entitlement by rewarding unearned achievements—i.e., "If you give somebody something for nothing, they'll want even more for less."

- **Prudent Negotiation:** In negotiations, draw upon Prudence to create sustainable agreements. This is what builds a sense of Justice, trust, and respect.

- **Merit:** Fair treatment doesn't always mean equal treatment. Justice means rewarding individuals based on their specific contributions and achievements.

- **Flexibility:** Be open to flexible arrangements for employees facing unique circumstances but ensure these decisions are made with Justice to all team members in mind.

- **Influence:** Given the state of younger generations, your role as a leader can instill a sense of Justice and other virtues they may not have been offered until arriving at a workplace setting. Wield your influence with wisdom.

- **A Virtuous Work Ethic:** The best way to create a productive work environment is to lead by example. Demonstrate a strong work ethic and a commitment to Justice.
- **Be Wary of HR Trends:** Challenge and critically assess popular trends that do not align with true principles of Justice. This will create a strong culture, not divide it further.
- **Use the One-Third Rule:** Identify the one-third who do not show promise or a willingness to grow. Hire, lead, and launch the remaining two-thirds into Giant status!

3

Fortitude: Do What You Don't Feel Like Doing

ortitude is essential for leaders. Nobody wants to be led by a fearful quitter. To be a Giant you need to be courageous, persevere, and suffer difficulties well. As simple as it may sound, mental health relies on this virtue. When we let our emotions dominate our intellect, we become mentally unstable. So, the one-two punch of Prudence and Fortitude are the bedrock for success and satisfaction. As we discussed, the third step in Prudence is **doing what is good**, and Fortitude is the thing that gets you to bring that action into its greatest potential.

There are two specific aspects of Fortitude and ways to build them. Additionally, there are two practical ways to build Fortitude in general:

- **Two Parts of Fortitude:**
    1. **Courage:** This is primarily obtained by introducing yourself to what causes fear in small doses. As the experiences build over time, the ability to handle the fears increases.

45

2. **Perseverance and Patience:** Whereas training in courage is a choice, perseverance and patience are usually, although not always, decisions that are forced upon us. Classically, this is described as the ability to "suffer well hardships in life."

- **Two Practical and Simple Ways to Learn Fortitude:**
  1. Do what you don't feel like doing, which is ultimately the key to success.
  2. Know that your problems are your friends.

FORTITUDE THROUGH COURAGE

An average person runs out of a burning building because he follows his fear. Firefighters, however, run into the building. They train to do things contrary to fear but still in accordance with reason. That is a great metaphor for leading Giants because Giants run toward what makes most people afraid. That action gets others to turn around and follow the courage of the Giant. This is the essence of Fortitude, which means being willing to engage the arduous. It's built over time, through training. If you wish to build fortitude through courage, then expose yourself—in small, manageable doses—to experiences that normally make you afraid. Then, over time, increase your exposure and you will build this incredible virtue. When you build courage by exposing yourself to things that previously scared you, you start to see a bigger picture emerge. Ultimately, Fortitude is the virtue that empowers soldiers to lead others in battle and to see past being wounded all the way to laying down their lives for a comrade. It's what gets business executives past the fear of being unpopular, therefore able to make bold decisions. It empowers financiers to make investments rather than only fear loss. Courage leads athletes to face rivals after building confidence from beating lesser opponents. It allows performers to take the big stage after many performances in smaller venues.

Courage is a crucial part of becoming a Giant and transforming others into Giants. Fortitude by way of courage exhibits strength, and strength is a major part of being influential. People with true Fortitude also have magnanimity, which gets them to desire excellence in great matters. The person who willfully prevents himself from being a Giant either never desires excellence in his life or desires it only in small things like mastering a video game. In a meeting, a person with Fortitude encourages others to seek great things and redirects them away from irrelevant matters. He helps diminish the fixation others have on things like the fear of competition and guides them to do quality work within their own organization. Conversely, a person who lacks Fortitude gets emotionally caught up in the weeds and fears things that are unlikely to ever manifest. The classic saying that "a coward dies a thousand deaths" applies to the person without Fortitude. It makes them weak, which repels followers.

Fortitude is guided by Prudence. Having the ability to follow right reason guides the prudent Giant and is the navigational device that points Fortitude in the right direction. That's why for the courageous firefighter, who has trained to fight fires, it is reasonable to enter a burning building, whereas for someone untrained, it would be unreasonable and imprudent. It allows us to align our emotions and our will with our intellect. Of course, there are urgent and surprising exceptions where a person acts courageously in an unchosen, unexpected setting. An example would be a parent, untrained in firefighting, who might enter a burning building to save his child. It's either love or the habit of courage he has trained in other areas that manifests in new circumstances like fending off an attacker. Prudence also guides people to Fortitude by helping them discern where to spend their energy. Am I cut out to be a firefighter, leader, or lawyer? Once the decision is made, Fortitude will be required to get past the fears that accompany virtually every new job and experience.

As a Leader of Giants, it is crucial for you to know what battles to pick and what deserves your energy. You have the ability as a human, within reasonable limits, to create any lifestyle, art, music, or business you desire. It's your responsibility to harness the power of Fortitude in the process of creating something good, true, and beautiful, something we'll cover more in chapter 5.

FORTITUDE THROUGH PERSEVERANCE AND PATIENCE

To understand the difference between courage and perseverance/patience, consider how, as I mentioned already, firefighters build courage by incrementally introducing themselves to what causes them fear. They do this deliberately, in manageable doses, with increased exposure, over long periods of time, expecting to someday be in an actual fire. When you watch their actions, it's easy to see Fortitude by way of courage. While there are some situations that require courage urgently and involuntarily, many decisions regarding courage are premeditated and optional. For example, should I be a public speaker or not? You also see Fortitude in someone who is willing to suffer difficult times gracefully over longer periods of time. This is the Fortitude of perseverance and patience.

A person faced with the decision to learn perseverance and patience usually has it forced upon them without his or her consent. For example, when a wife finds out her husband will need to endure a long cancer treatment, she decides how to react. Does she stay by his side and suffer well with him? Or does this sadness make her run away so she doesn't have to endure this difficult situation? We see examples of both types of people. One with the virtue of Fortitude, who gains your admiration by staying by his side. Or the other who abandons him, which even if you understand, you likely don't respect it. Giants suffer hardships well, with little complaining. They can be sad, frustrated, and lonely but they rise above these emotions empowered by love, which fuels perseverance and patience.

TWO PRACTICAL AND SIMPLE WAYS TO LEARN FORTITUDE

Concepts like the virtue of Fortitude can be easy to describe but difficult to learn unless you can approach them in simple terms. Over the years, I have learned that there are two ways to develop Fortitude:

1. Do what you don't feel like doing, which is ultimately the key to success.
2. Know that your problems are your friends.

Do What You Don't Feel Like Doing

When I was in my 20s, my businesses were successful, so I occasionally had people ask me, "What's the key to success?" As a young man, I had no idea how to answer that question, so I went on and on with enough words to fill a book. In my 30s, I narrowed it down to a paragraph or two. By the time I hit 40, I knew the irrefutable key to success: **do what you don't feel like doing**. At the time, I had no idea this little phrase was a usable but radically simplified way of saying Fortitude.

At the end of the day, if you go to bed saying, "I did only what I felt like doing," you've probably had an unfulfilling day. But if you accomplished all that you didn't feel like doing, you'll be pleasantly exhausted, excited for the next day. As a CEO, I learned my satisfaction hinged on doing the things I didn't feel like doing, and my success came from teaching people in the organization to do the same. This is where I learned the importance of not only leading Giants, but helping ordinary people become Giants.

Fortitude ensures firmness in difficulties and consistency in the pursuit of good. It is cultivated through enduring challenges and overcoming obstacles with bravery and resilience. Having courage is not about being fearless; it's about facing your fears to fulfill a noble cause. That sounds big and heroic but on most days it's very subtle.

Before I go further, I want to make something clear. Doing what you don't *feel* like doing does not always mean doing what you don't *like* doing. Many of the things we don't feel like doing at a given moment, we actually like at other times. You may like working out but just don't feel like it today. You may like your job but just not want to go in today. You hopefully like being kind to your family and friends, but sometimes you are in a bad mood and you don't feel like it. This is an important distinction because success does not require exclusively doing things you don't like to do, albeit that's part of it.

Good behaviors almost always require at least mild Fortitude, and good behaviors don't disappear on vacations or the weekend. Success comes from tiny victories such as immediately getting out of bed, working out anyway, or making a healthy breakfast even, and especially, when you don't feel like it. Even if you do all that, you may not feel like going to work, but you do it anyway. Then, you may not feel like being nice to that person who sent you that bothersome email, but you do it anyway. You might have a tight schedule, so you don't feel like calling your significant other just to say something encouraging. But knowing they need support, you do it anyway. The day that you go to bed doing things that you didn't feel like doing, you'll feel amazing. You will say to yourself, "You know what? I had a difficult day, but it was awesome. Let's do it again tomorrow." What makes you great and builds virtue in your life is to do difficult things with gratitude. The cultivation of Fortitude can initially be challenging, especially if you haven't yet mastered Prudence and Justice. It is literally impossible to have Fortitude without working on these two preceding virtues, so focus on all of them to make it possible.

Bravely seeing things for what they truly are is also important. For instance, you might need to start saving for your child's upcoming college days, but you don't know where to start. You might be afraid that you won't ever be able to afford it. That fear makes you run from the effort. Then, a friend points out that you spend $15 per day on Starbucks, racking up $5,500 per year in caffeine and calories. Over the next 15 years, that's $82,000, not including interest, which could make that number double. This awareness triggers Prudence and Justice; therefore, despite the fact that you don't feel like saving that money and you can't resist the venti, creamy, peppermint-pumped coffee and pastry, you make the right choice. That choice also requires Temperance, which is the virtue that grows out of Fortitude, in the same way Prudence and Justice precede Fortitude.

While it is seemingly unheroic to forgo Starbucks for a day, it is absolutely heroic to save for your child's education. Day by day, bit by bit, that sacrifice builds the muscles of virtue. Fortitude always has a target or a goal, like an end zone. In this analogy, your child's education is the end zone and avoiding Starbucks is like dodging opponents who want to tackle you. Over time, you accept the competition is there and give much more thought to the end zone than you do to being tackled.

Embodying Fortitude, you'll find yourself willing to enter a conversation to help a cause, whereas before you feared offending someone. Patients who go through routine testing often talk about how they feared needles when they first went to the doctor, but over time, nothing scares them anymore. This is a forced virtue of Fortitude, but nonetheless an example of how repetitive exposure to doing what you don't feel like doing creates unforeseen strength.

Many examples of exercising Fortitude have a spillover effect on our lives. The Starbucks example not only allows your child to go to college, it also enhances your health, refines your budget, and becomes the gateway to Temperance, the next virtue that creates happiness in life at an entirely new level. When you shift your actions to accomplish something greater than your own desires, doing what you don't feel like doing becomes a mechanism for feeling grateful, purposeful, and driven. Rather than wasting time debating whether or not you should do the right thing, you will take action quickly and see things through to completion.

Know That Your Problems Are Your Friends

Imagine that you've just arrived on vacation to a tropical island. The first day, you're in awe, thinking, *I could live here forever. Maybe I should just leave my problems behind and take a simple job like working at that tiki bar.* The next day, your excitement continues as you watch the bartender living the dream, overlooking the beach. He meets interesting people and gets to do as he pleases all day. What a life! By the third day, a thought creeps in: *As great as this is, could I really stay idle here for the rest of my life? You know, I think so! It's so peaceful here.* At some point, the timing of which would vary for most of us, you start questioning if you're going to need the full vacation. The relaxation has been restorative, but time moves so slowly that you may get antsy. Given enough time, the charm diminishes, the tiki bar's bottomless piña coladas make you sick, and you absolutely have to get home. You can't wait for your flight to get back to your responsibilities so you can be productive.

When you stop being productive or building toward something, it affects your well-being. Stagnation isn't beneficial, nor is it what you should aim for in periods of recreation; you need growth and engagement in your life to thrive. Stagnation is why so many people's health rapidly declines after retirement. No matter what kind of team you lead or are part of, if you have a family, or if you're learning to lead yourself, you must learn to embrace the fact that your problems are your friends. Doing what we don't feel like doing is about perpetual self-improvement, sacrifice, and creating value. It's more than that, however. It's how to generate more satisfaction and happiness in life. If you fail to recognize that your problems are your friends, you'll have a hard time. That's not to say your problems are things you want to keep around, but that solving them is what gives them meaning.

Every single job that's ever been created in the world was created to solve a problem. Sometimes, shysters manufacture problems that shouldn't be created only to solve them by using people. But outside of those nefarious individuals and companies, the foundation of business and leadership is centered on solving good problems in the most efficient, genius, and effective ways possible.

Just like recognizing a problem that needs to be solved leads to success in business, identifying the significance of our personal problems is pivotal. Overcoming these challenges shapes us and hones our virtues. Many lottery winners often face financial ruin, and some even commit suicide, within five to ten years of winning. Why? Because when handed vast sums, the need to maintain personal discipline dissipates because their primary problems go away. Sudden gains of fortune through winning the lottery, selling a business, or getting an inheritance changes people's lifestyle dynamic. When someone who is not virtuous wakes up in the morning, no longer faced with the "problems" of food, shelter, clothing, or even luxury habits that are a product of or need to be maintained via hard work, they usually self-generate or perpetuate problems. Drugs, alcohol, poor choices in friends, vanity purchases, and the like creep in. This can happen unconsciously, but it is simply filling a need to solve new problems. So, we can either solve problems that are present and productive or create problems that are new and destructive. Either way, we are wired to solve problems and we will always have them.

Generally, those who've built wealth versus just getting a windfall stand a better chance of maintaining and capitalizing on it because the journey of building a business instills certain disciplines and virtues, though this isn't always the case. Sometimes, there are the startup unicorns or the one-hit-wonders who earn massive amounts without developing the maturity to handle it, leading to personal and professional downfall. When the speed of prosperity moves at a faster pace than virtue grows, be careful. Even those who've cultivated virtues while building businesses can see those virtues erode when faced with sudden success. It's crucial to understand that your problems, big or small, give life meaning.

A CAUTION ABOUT FALSE COURAGE

A common misconception about Leaders of Giants is that they never give up. This is far from true, and it is a vice counter to Fortitude called excessiveness. It's played out in the excessive pursuit of a bad idea. The difference between a Leader of Giants and a leader of nanos is that the former knows when to quit, pivot, or redirect. This is why Prudence must guide the way to Fortitude.

I have witnessed many colleagues and friends pursue bad ideas (usually fueled by ego) that had no chance of success. Ultimately, some of them lost everything. Acknowledging the necessity of sometimes quitting is often shunned by the motivational gurus of today who say, "Never give up," and "You can do or be anything you want to be." Those are good ideas very often. It's true that some things we should never quit. But taken to the extreme, they are poisonous ideas that are said either in ignorance of a circumstance or as a tool to manipulate by selling false hope. On one side of the spectrum, failure happens because a person lacks Fortitude and quits too easily. On the other side of the spectrum, the pursuit of a bad idea is the reason for failure. But there is a middle ground that takes up most of the space. In that middle ground, you will find that mediocre ideas can become great if you know when to pivot or what to change.

The guiding lights for knowing when to stay the course, quit, or pivot are found in Prudence and Justice. Then, when things get difficult, they are fulfilled through Fortitude. Building Fortitude as courage is usually a long, slow, and difficult process, but it is always worth it.

LEAD AS A GIANT BY KNOWING THE HUMAN NATURE WE ALL SHARE

If you want to lead Giants, you need to reinforce good behaviors. To do so, you must also recognize when Fortitude is in deficit. This is paramount in developing Fortitude in your team. As I mentioned in the chapter on Justice, currently there are way more soft people (the antithesis of Fortitude) in the world than at any other time. Rather than complain about it, you need to teach strength via Fortitude. That's the way you transform ordinary people into Giants.

It starts by recognizing magnanimous behaviors. When a team member sets out and accomplishes an excellent thing, reward them with praise and gratitude. Publicly share stories not only of accomplishment but of sincere effort. Remember, Fortitude is active even before the end is met. Be careful to pay close attention to the way human nature can incline people to take dubious shortcuts so you don't accidentally reinforce bad behaviors. Sadly, recognizing the wrong things can turn ordinary people into nanos.

All my children are now adults, but when one of my sons was in high school, he was watching TV in the middle of the day. I asked what he was doing, and he responded accurately that he was watching TV. Predicting a motivational message from me, he got ahead of it and said, "I know the key to success is doing what you don't feel like doing, and believe me, I really don't feel like watching TV. So, I've decided to just muscle through it." He intercepted my speech and manipulated the circumstances to make me laugh. It was funny, and it shed light on his budding understanding of responsibility and the nuances of commitment.

At times, we all manipulate ourselves or others with self-justification, which is one of the greatest enemies of Fortitude. Being aware of this as a leader is important. Employees who aren't committed often think their manipulations are sophisticated enough to pass a test of scrutiny. However, those who do this don't realize how common and easily recognizable their actions are, such as:

- **Overstating Work Hours:** They might come in early and leave late, making it seem like they're working long hours. However, they're likely spending a lot of that time on non-work-related activities.
- **Busy Appearance:** Always appearing busy—lots of open tabs, piles of papers, or always in a meeting when they, in fact, might not be accomplishing much at all.
- **Email Time Stamps:** Sending emails at night or early in the morning to give the impression of working outside regular hours.
- **Imprudent Delegation:** Passing on tasks they could and should handle themselves to appear more senior or busier than they are.
- **Frequent Breaks:** Taking many short breaks with the excuse of needing to think, while using the time unproductively.
- **Misrepresenting Skills:** Claiming they need to attend a workshop or course to learn a specific skill they already possess or someone else can/should handle.
- **Playing the Victim:** Discussing personal problems or issues to gain sympathy and leniency on work tasks.
- **Hoarding Information:** Keeping certain information to themselves so they become the "go-to" person, making them seem indispensable.

- **Credit Snatching:** Taking credit for a colleague's work or idea and presenting it as their own.
- **Vague Updates:** Giving ambiguous updates on projects to buy more time or to avoid revealing a lack of progress.

These manipulations are ways people sail through work without actually doing anything arduous. They are ways to fake virtue without authentically committing to the tasks at hand. While some manipulations are harmless or even humorous, those listed are detrimental to organizational culture and are grounds for you to consider the future of their employment.

If you find yourself doing any of these, know that it's common. However, anything you do that's out of integrity will be detrimental to your influence as a leader, as well as deplete your personal and organizational resources. The important thing here is that as you build Fortitude in your own life—aka you learn to do what you don't feel like doing—you'll quickly start to recognize excuses and false virtues in others. Understanding human nature, and that all actions are either that of vice or virtue, is key to your success as a Leader of Giants.

GIANT TAKEAWAYS

Fortitude is the willingness to engage the arduous, yet is satisfied and able to rest when it reaches its target. A key difference between a Leader of Giants and a leader of nanos is that the former knows when to quit, pivot, or redirect.

The irrefutable key to success is this: do what you don't feel like doing. To implement this into your own life, starting right now, you need to do these two things:

1. **Understand Human Nature:** All actions are either that of vice or virtue.
2. **Accept That Your Problems Are Your Friends:** That's not to say your problems are things you want to keep around, but rather, solving your problems, big or small, gives life meaning. So, you can either solve problems that are present and productive or create problems that stem from destructive circumstances.

Remember, what makes you great and builds virtue in your life is to do difficult things with a grateful heart.

4

Temperance: Genuine Fulfillment Comes from Self-Control

"I loved the way my boss had no self-control," said nobody, ever.

MODERATION IS KEY BUT ELUSIVE

Temperance is the virtue that moderates our desire for pleasure—simply put, it's self-control. In the widest sense, Temperance regulates all forms of enjoyment that come from increasing your inherent mental and physical power. Through self-mastery you can gain introspection and discipline in the other Cardinal Virtues, which, with Temperance, provides control over your drives, passions, and appetites. This allows you to harmonize your internal desires with the external world. Doing so fosters individual well-being and also opens your full capacity to contribute to the good of others. The opposite is also true. Practical examples where people harm themselves or others because of a lack of Temperance would be things such as getting drunk at a company event or cheating on a spouse with a colleague. These things have nothing to do with leadership or making good business decisions, yet they can destroy your influence and business, not to mention your soul and the hearts of your loved ones. The challenge is that when it comes to our passions, we must be somewhat subjective, unlike the other virtues that are easier to measure, like Justice. If I take $20 from you, I owe you $20. It's pretty simple. But when it comes to other pleasures like food, it's more complex. Since you will always need to eat, you need to learn how much is too much, and that is where Temperance is required.

There are two simple questions to ask yourself to develop Temperance:

- Do I really need this (drink, interaction, attention, etc.)? And why am I seeking it?
- Will it make me the best version of myself or a worse version?

DO I REALLY NEED THIS? AND WHY AM I SEEKING IT?

Remember, a basic rule for becoming a Giant is to be in the process of mastering yourself before you expect the same of others. So, as you ask yourself this question, you should make assessments about the collective level of Temperance in your team. Simple questions can be so powerful that, to a certain degree, they require no answer to understand because your gut tells you without the need for audible articulation. Almost everyone can remember a moment when their passions began taking control of them, but they stopped themselves by asking simple questions like, "Why am I seeking this?" or "Do I really need this?" When you fail to adhere to your conscience, you regret it. When you obey, you will be grateful.

Here are a few simple questions leaders are wise to ask themselves to identify the need to improve their Temperance:

60

- Should I really comment on this topic in the meeting? Am I really contributing or just wanting to feel important and acknowledged?
- Did I cut that person off in an unfair manner when they were speaking (which combines Justice with Temperance)?
- Am I impulsively doing the work of others that they can do on their own because I lack self-control, ironically by being controlling?
- Am I getting my work done on time or are there other passions (online meandering, etc.) that are preventing me from managing my priorities?
- Am I drinking too much, oversleeping, eating, or intaking things that inhibit my performance at work?

There are many more questions you can ask yourself. As you learn more about yourself, you will learn to make observations in others. Leading people past their own lack of Temperance is not easy. In some ways, the topics aren't your business. Yet, in other ways, when the bad habits of your team members hinder their performance, they become your concern. The challenge is that you can't always ask the questions you may need to ask someone to determine if their passions are inhibiting their performance. The questions might be too personal or too embarrassing. So, you may just need to keep the focus on the performance and say something like, "I'm not sure what is getting in the way, but something is interfering with your results. If you need help or want to talk, I'm available to listen and to help as best I can. If you don't ask for help, I will assume that everything is okay and that your performance will return to where it needs to be ASAP."

WILL THIS MAKE ME THE BEST VERSION OF MYSELF OR A WORSE VERSION?

Like the other Cardinal Virtues, Temperance has many sub-virtues within it. When you master them, you become the best version of yourself, but if you don't, you become a worse version. It really is that simple. In fact, the sub-virtues of Temperance are a great summary of what most of us want or demand in others when we expect them to be the best versions of themselves. A person who has Temperance will have more humility, patience, forgiveness, authenticity, restrained anger, and hospitality. Ironically, most of us expect or demand these virtues in others, even more than we expect to uphold them for ourselves. So, in keeping with the theme of this book, you must develop them in your own life if you expect those around you to have them.

Ask yourself when you engage your passions, "Will this make me the best version of myself or a worse version?" To help yourself be honest about the answer, you could put it another way: "If my (friend, colleague, spouse, or whoever else makes sense) acted this same way, would I approve or be upset?" This is a tremendous way to ferret out self-justification, which is at the core of submitting to bad ideas surrounding passions.

DON'T BE ASHAMED OF SHAME

Unfortunately, Temperance is under attack in today's world. A prime example of this is that shame, which plays an important role for a person to develop Temperance, is ridiculed. Shame is a feeling of embarrassment or humiliation that arises from the perception of having done something dishonorable, immoral, or improper. While shaming someone with an intent to hurt them is obviously wrong, if someone feels shameful for what they've done, it's simply information that can be used to do better the next time. The confusion around shame is that when we feel it and don't have the connectedness with ourselves or others to process it, it can leave us feeling stuck and negatively identified with what we've done. Both guilt and shame are helpful teachers, but only if we know how to process them instead of being ashamed of feeling shame—a vicious cycle that helps nobody.

Cutting shame out of your life is like cutting out nerve endings that cause pain to warn you of even greater danger. Knowing to pull your hand away from a hot flame so you don't get burned is not something you want to get rid of. Likewise, if you avoid feeling your shame, you will cut off the virtue of Temperance and you will get burned in other ways. Telling someone that a bad behavior is good or healthy when it isn't is not good, kind, just, or anything positive. If someone is morbidly overweight and you're a doctor, you need to counsel them to lose weight. Being afraid to make them feel bad about overeating and placing that fear above their health is wrong. So, from a leadership perspective, you need to have the courage or Fortitude to help someone develop their Temperance. If you have an employee who talks too much in a meeting, be kind about it but tell him so the meetings can be more productive. It's the behavior of the person that causes the real shame, not you, even if you're the one to mention it.

We all have to face the consequences of our behaviors, and leaders have an important role in helping shape individuals laden with vice.

DON'T BE SEAWEED

A practical example of an intemperate person is a manager who had a good idea prior to a staff meeting. The idea may not be unique and may be the exact same idea shared by other peers. When the topic comes up and the team agrees to carry out the idea, he can't resist saying, "That was my idea!" He needs the recognition, even if others also had the same idea. The funny thing is that he can't see how weak this makes him look. Nobody in the room thinks, *Oh yes, glad he said that. He's smart. Let's all recognize him for his great idea.* A person who lacks Prudence might say something to try to make him feel better, but internally they think, *Who cares whose idea it was? We're all working hard at this and there's no time for a credit taker.* Ironically, the credit taker is most often also the blamer. They have a penchant for saying, "I told you so," when things go wrong. In my experience, they almost never warn you of an upcoming bad decision despite their "I told you so" claim. The lack of humility demonstrated by this person stems from a lack of Temperance.

People who lack Temperance also lack at least one of the other Cardinal Virtues, which is why they are often quite unhappy and tend to struggle with anxiety. The anxiety stems from knowing that they are like seaweed moving back and forth with the current, unable to take a stand against the waves. They wonder in fear what the next day will hold. They are subject to the classic pattern of hopping and skipping on the way to their sins but crawling back from them in sorrow.

Lacking Temperance causes self-centeredness, which is why it always accompanies narcissists. They don't have the ability to regulate anger, yet they don't like themselves when they lose their temper, which makes them even more volatile. At times they can be hospitable, but for the most part, hospitality requires not partaking in the pleasure that the subjects of hospitality are experiencing. This makes it difficult to maintain a hospitable disposition at home, at work, and in all areas of life.

SIMPLE WAYS TO BUILD TEMPERANCE

So, what's the solution? As you build on the Cardinal Virtues, you need to become more diagnostic. If you recognize that a person can't make a decision, it's easy to see they lack Prudence, and since that comes first, they inherently lack the other Cardinal Virtues. But a person who lacks Temperance may not fully lack the other virtues, so getting to the root of their shortcomings is important. In other words, it is difficult to jump to building Temperance by itself if you lack the foundation of the other three virtues before it.

Clearly, the steps to becoming a person with Temperance include learning Prudence, Justice, and Fortitude. The silver lining is that once you have learned these three virtues, you are very inclined to build Temperance with momentum from the others. In other words, Temperance comes more naturally when you master the previous three. However, it takes considerable effort to master it.

Here are a few steps to get there:

- **Establish routines.**

  Not having a routine is almost always associated with people who lack temperance. Setting order in your life by way of routine has a dramatically generalizing impact. When you set a specific time each day for exercise, study, prayer, or the like, you begin fortifying the characteristics that ground you when tempted.

- **Fast.**

  Yes, literally give up something small that you normally like or has become a vice. Skip dessert, drinks, or a meal. Because Temperance has to do with the passions, you can learn it bit by bit by reducing your slavery to passions. It is truly amazing how making the intentional choice to skip the French fries, or even better to skip entire meals, can build into a greater sense of Temperance in other areas of your life. Our minds make broad connections from specific experiences; thus, our willpower can be strengthened through specific acts like fasting.

- **Bite your tongue.**

  That's right; just say less, more often. Rather than thinking too hard about what to say or not to say, just say less. By practicing this, you will begin to recognize how often you want to speak just to satisfy your ego versus having something of value to add. Over time, you will develop the classic wisdom of thinking before you speak. It will likely be regulated by the idea that you should only speak if you have something to add. This applies socially and relationally, as well as professionally.

- **Practice empathy.**
  Being empathetic means having the ability to see things from the perspective of those around you and feel their pain or pleasure as if it were your own. Unless you suffer from narcissistic personality disorder, or other related psychological disorders, you will naturally be inclined to be compassionate to others. How do your passions make your significant other feel? Do they put doubts in their mind or break trust? Do you embarrass loved ones or coworkers because of boastfulness or attention seeking? Empathy for others helps regulate a lack of Temperance. You must practice it to master it.

Bringing Temperance into your organization is challenging because Prudence, Justice, and Fortitude must be cultivated and underway for a person to develop self-control. The best way I have found to do this is by highlighting people's successes. The more often you recognize people for authentically portraying any of the virtues, the more others will want to be recognized for the same. For example, if you are a sales manager and one of your team members postponed a golf date in order to make a sale, you'd be wise to praise him for that sacrifice. Yet you must be cautious because Temperance is something that can be misunderstood. A common misunderstanding would be to perceive all people who work hard as having Temperance. While a soldier who is deployed should be recognized for his or her familial sacrifice, recognizing someone who chooses to never go home to their family because they unnecessarily decide to be at work late can send the wrong message. "Bob never sees his family because he burns the midnight oil with us, and I want to thank him." That message can come off as though you think work is more important than family. This may create a lack of trust, so pay close attention to who, what, and how you recognize.

Just because Bob is hard at work and not slacking off on the beach or avoiding his family doesn't mean he isn't a slave to his passions. We all have different passions. For some people, work is their passion, and they fail to regulate it, therefore neglecting important things and people around them. Justifying your preferred methods without Temperance for theirs is not a way to develop the virtue in your organization. If you're the leader and you're a "workaholic," don't ask your team to be the same. If you think I'm wrong on this, I just ask that you keep reading until you get to chapter 8, and I promise I'll say things there that will surprise you.

Additionally, working too much is bad for you, bad for your family, and even bad for business. There's a classic moral axiom that *the end does not justify the means*. So, if you desire high productivity by being a workaholic and demanding that from others, you have justified the means by creating vice. People resent it when you make them choose their job over their families. Obviously, there are times and seasons where we all must work more than is typical, but sound logic and reason (Prudence and Justice) regulates when those times make sense and when they are overkill.

You need to be objective about the virtues, and not try to bend other people's experience to your biased lack of virtue. If you drink five drinks a day and convince others to do the same, it does not make you normal or healthy. It just makes others unhealthy with you. So, cultivate each one of the virtues honestly if you want your team to do the same. When you do, you'll be living with the Four Superpowers of a Leader, which not only makes you a titan of your industry—a Giant—but also brings influence, power, and purpose into all areas of your life.

GIANT TAKEAWAYS

Once you harness each of the previous Cardinal Virtues, Temperance is that which helps you desire and actually achieve excellence in your life. Additionally, the sub-virtues of Temperance are a great summary of what most of us want or demand in others: humility, patience, forgiveness, authenticity, restrained anger, and hospitality. On the other hand, people who lack Temperance are often quite unhappy and tend to struggle with anxiety, making good leadership nearly impossible.

A person who lacks Temperance also lacks Prudence, Justice, and Fortitude—and they're easy to spot because they live by these two recognizable mottos: "It's good enough," or "It's the least I can do." To avoid these behaviors, there are three surprising ways to gain Temperance:

- **Fasting:** Starve your vice and feed virtue. Because Temperance has to do with the passions, you can learn it bit by bit by reducing your slavery to passions.
- **Biting Your Tongue:** You should only speak if you have something to add. So, say less, more often.
- **Practicing Empathy:** Empathy for others helps regulate a lack of Temperance; it's the sub-virtue that will attract Giants (victory-minded people) and repel nanos (victim-minded people).

Ask yourself these questions, and write down your answers somewhere you can revisit them later:

- How well am I implementing each of the four Cardinal Virtues in my life?
- What vice do I have that decreases my quality of life or that of someone I love?
- What committed actions am I doing daily to overcome that vice?

SECTION 2

Big Bang Leadership: How to Rapidly Expand Your Influence

When building any organization, culture will be the ultimate reason for long-term success or failure. Of course, the best place to begin when starting an organization or new initiative is with good questions. When you understand the Cardinal Virtues, you gain a much fuller understanding of the value of questions, how to form them, and how to answer them effectively. There are four crucial organizational questions you must answer to build a great team and establish a strong culture:

1. For what purpose was this (the company, the product, the service, the meeting agenda, etc.) made?
2. What priorities should we focus on?
3. How will we go about it (broken down by tasks, timelines, and people)?
4. What will we do to stay on pace, finish on time, and measure our progress (aka know that we completed the goal)?

These questions, in one way or another, are commonly known. Unfortunately, they are haphazardly asked and/or never answered in most organizations. If the people asking them fail to cultivate the Cardinal Virtues in their lives, they will fall short in their ability to answer them. They will also fail to ask related questions that good answers to these four inspire. Building the Cardinal Virtues in your life is the first step to developing what it takes to come up with good answers.

The second step is to harness the Transcendental Desires of goodness, truth, beauty, and unity. The Transcendental Desires are universal desires that all humans possess. When you understand them, you can use them to amplify the quality of the questions asked and the answers that ensue. In fact, as bold as it may sound, every company that has ever accomplished anything good has tapped into these desires, even if they haphazardly or ignorantly applied them. Conversely, every organization that has failed did so because it ignored each of these universal desires. This section of the book will show you what they are and how to deliberately apply them, and answer the four questions that are essential for cultural health. The effect is like sharpening and heating a knife before cutting cold butter. You will also see how each one of these questions is muscled by one or more of the Cardinal Virtues. Therefore, the Cardinal Virtues and the Transcendentals work together.

The rest of this section will provide insights as to how Giants positively influence the maximum number of people they can, in the shortest period of time. Doing so takes thought, effort, strategy, and execution. Leadership and influence are predicated on action. You lead people somewhere and you influence people to do things. Neither leadership nor influence are passive. They move people. This next section will show you the necessary desires and strategies to create action.

To attract, retain, and develop top talent, leaders must live and act in certain ways. You can't give what you don't have, so if you want to influence others, you must first be influential. If you want a great culture, you must have the attributes that a great culture requires, which means you will act in accordance with them. After diving into the Transcendental Desires, the rest of the second section of *Leading Giants* will shed light on the ways to expand your influence by attracting, retaining, developing, and launching those you lead into greatness.

As you continue, I want you to consider that there's a lot of confusion about what makes a genuine leader (Giant) versus a mere influencer. In the world of social media today, people confuse "influencers" with influential leaders. They are vastly different. To truly be a leader, you must make consequential decisions, not just spew out ideas that may or may not be true, may or may not be effective, or may or may not be damaging. Leaders live and die with the actual results they create, and those results are created with and through the people they lead.

Influencers are like consultants. They say things and leave their subjects to live or die with the decisions they make. When it comes to organizational leadership, leaders have authority over the people who follow them. Influencers, however, have sway, not direct authority. The difference is not subtle. That means organizational leaders are held accountable to the results of their followers. Influencers are not held to the same level of accountability. Higher levels of virtue, savvy, and intellect are all required of a true leader.

Some chapters are counterintuitive, such as the chapter dispelling the notion that positive results require long hours. Other chapters will center on a blend of philosophical and strategic approaches to rapidly expand your influence. Lastly, there are both preventative and protective ideas offered in this section, such as the way cultural ideas take shape and being aware of communication dos and don'ts.

Each chapter was written with your long-term success in mind, yet will also give you rapid expansion and immediate usefulness.

A Hidden Power to Influence and Motivate Comes from the Transcendentals: Unity, Truth, Beauty, and Goodness

I n many ways, this is the cardinal chapter of the book, meaning everything hinges on whether you build a united, true, beautiful, and good organization. These ancient principles are timeless and instrumental to the modern context of building, scaling, and leading a business. All organizations flourish only to the degree that they have Transcendental qualities, but most leaders are not intentional about their importance. These Transcendentals, originally described by Plato, are useful in conjunction with the four Cardinal Virtues from the first section of this book, and as such, they are the ultimate ideals to harness and enact.

Transcendental Desires are universal. They are hardwired into our human nature and every human wants them, without limits. Nobody thinks: *I've had enough goodness; please serve me up some badness now. No thanks to all that beauty; I've had enough. I'm tired of all that truth; please deceive me now.* Or, *This unity and cohesion are tiresome; let's create division and chaos now.* Because these are universal desires, they have a universal set of mirroring repulsions or antonyms. Badness, lies, ugliness, and division are all things that repel humans unless they have developed a warped conscience, in which case you don't want to attract them to your organization anyway. Building an organization that is united, true, good, and beautiful is a sure way to attract and retain great talent and long-term customers and clients.

After I write briefly about each Transcendental desire, I will show you how they and the Cardinal Virtues impact each of the four organizational essential questions I wrote about in the introduction to this section.

UNITY

Unity is sometimes left off the list of Transcendentals, but it is very important to include as you build a great organization. I will cover it comprehensively in the next chapter due to its relevance to your organizational culture. Yet, in summary, this Transcendental desire is about cohesion and alignment, first and foremost within yourself, and then infused into the organization you lead.

When building and leading a company, it's essential to have a singular, unified vision. Today, forced diversity is an enemy of unity. Actual unity is a product of virtue, merit, and alignment, and it is the foundation of any healthy culture, regardless of size or influence.

Being a united organization is more than just maintaining an image; it's about ensuring that every employee, from top leadership to the new hires, aligns with the core mission. Unity is not just a strategic advantage but a cultural one that begets an even greater strategy and vice versa.

When employees feel they are part of something bigger, they are more likely to rise up, take initiative, and emerge as leaders.

As I share in the next chapter, if your number one goal is to recruit the best people, you will likely end up diverse and united. And if you don't, it will be because some people, of their own accord, are just not interested in what you do. Forcing them to partake in what you do simply to hit numbers is not just or good.

TRUTH

The truth is utterly attractive but lies repel people and make your gut uneasy. When you lie, you also get uneasy, which is why lie detectors work. When you tell the truth and hear the truth, you feel better. We all desire truth. It's only dysfunction that warps that desire. Therefore, to lead a healthy and motivated team, keeping truth at the core of your culture is imperative. The truth retains great people, whereas lies repel them.

In chapter 1, I shared the three steps to mastering a decision. These were to **desire what is good**, **know what is real**, and **do what is good**. For you to desire, know, and do what is good and real means you and everyone around you is operating in truth. Truth is the correspondence or agreement between a statement or belief and actual reality. While truth can be proven via data or evidence, there's something credible to the idea that we can feel what's true through intuition or gut instincts.

It's worth noting that contemporary philosophy and postmodern thought, which has penetrated the business world, challenges the notion of objective truth. Some argue that truth is subjective only and that there are only "personal truths." They contend that truth is influenced by cultural, historical, and individual factors, making it difficult to arrive at a single, objective truth about anything. While I understand the confusion regarding this perspective, it's entirely ridiculous when it's thought through. If I prefer tomatoes and I express that preference, it remains a truthful statement, not just "my truth." More practically, if the data shows that your marketing idea was not liked by the consumers, you can't have "your truth" that says they like it and still be right. If you presented that to the team, you'd be fired relatively quickly.

Arguing that there is no ultimate truth implies that this assertion is true. As you can see, this perspective is self-refuting and doesn't stand up to scrutiny. I admire those who operate in search of and in reverence to what is true, knowing it can and should be found. The pursuit of truth is the greatest sign of strength. The denial of truth is the greatest sign of weakness. If you don't desire and embrace the truth, you are weak.

The truth is the most simple, clear, and direct explanation for all things. Yet if you entertain the notion that no ultimate truth exists, you can never be a strong leader, and that weakness opens the door for you to be subject to manipulations. Conversely, the pursuit of truth makes you strong but isn't an excuse to forgo empathy and humility. Why? Because it risks morphing into authoritarianism. Both conservative and liberal ideologies can descend into tyranny, and they find their way into companies quite often.

The only way societies can have harmony is by having a common understanding of truth. If I say I am sitting on a chair, it should mean I am sitting on a chair. If everyone interprets "I am sitting on a chair" differently, language itself becomes useless. When people debate truths, they do it to come to the truth on a matter. So, debating if truth exists or not is silly for a person who denies truth. He would lose the debate if he were correct, and, of course, he loses it if he is wrong. It used to be that certain matters were settled with other disciplines to find truths, such as science. However, far too many people today have politicized science and other disciplines to advance agendas, therefore making data hard to believe.

A recent survey found that Americans "find truth" or reject it in the following ways: "The most common notion is that God is the basis of truth—but it was a minority of only four out of ten adults (42%). Another four out of ten believe that either inner certainty (16%), scientific proof (15%), tradition (5%), or public consensus (4%) leads to knowing truth. The remaining two out of every ten adults said that either there is no such thing as truth (5%) or that they do not know the basis of truth (13%)."[1] This shows that 18% of people don't believe in truth at all, and that percentage nearly doubles in younger people entering the workforce. A full 58% of people can't agree on where truth comes from, which creates a huge leadership challenge when it comes to getting people to align for a mission.

As a Giant you must know, on your own, how to identify the truth and equally how to identify people and ideas that are not true. The good news is that there are several ways to do so, of which I will focus on two. The first is to be humble. Pride clouds judgment, as does bias. Pride also blocks learning, which is essential to disseminating the truth on matters. The second way is also powerful, and when things are debatable, it's the gold standard. That is by using the law of non-contradiction. "The law of non-contradiction states that nothing can both be and not be at the same time and in the same relationship. Put more formally, 'A' cannot be 'B' at the same time and in the same relationship" (socraticdictum.com).

The reason some people tell you that you can't know truth is simply to overpower you. If you can't know truth, then you can't point out their errors, plain and simple. This allows them to act any way they want without hindrance. Imagine having a roommate who steals your wallet but tells you it's his wallet because that's his truth. While most people are not that brazen, even slight degrees of that way of thinking are damaging to your team. As simple as it sounds, if a person says you can't know truth, they mean you can't know *any* truth; otherwise, the statement is false to begin with. That simple example is why you can't work with people who don't believe in truth. They will not hold themselves accountable. They can't be humble, either, because humility relies on a truthful examination of oneself. If they lie, cheat, steal, etc., but say "their truth" is that they are honest and trustworthy, they won't change, and they will be angry with you if you challenge them.

In business, you must be honest about the capabilities of your products or services. As businesses scale, leaders often face the temptation to inflate numbers or overpromise to attract new talent or increase sales. Resisting this and maintaining a commitment to the truth ensures long-term trust and credibility. As a virtue-based leader, embracing truth means being transparent, admitting mistakes, and being genuine in all interactions. When a leader commits to the truth, it helps empower employees to rise up as leaders themselves. This begets Giants leading Giants.

GOODNESS

It's been said that the enemy of great is good. There have rarely been wiser words. "It's good enough" as a mentality can crush performance. However, there is a time when good enough makes sense, and as a Giant, you need to know the difference. However, when it comes to the Transcendental desire for goodness, you must understand it more practically. Goodness has perfection as its aim. Goodness happens when something is created and used perfectly for its intended purpose. That means it realizes the purpose of the one who created it. If you hold a meeting to solve a production problem, and the meeting solves the problem, that's good. If you only discuss the social lives of the attendees, it's a bad meeting. The distinguishing difference is that the former did what it was designed to do, for the purpose it was designed for by you, the creator.

Goodness is related to Prudence and Justice. If someone doesn't desire what is good or know what is real, or if they pursue an unjust mission, then it can't be truly good, even if it is used for its intended purpose. For example, consider an individual who intends to make a plan to trip someone to cause injury just for laughs. The successful creation and execution of the plan, meaning it fulfilled the purpose of its creator, is still not good because its end is bad. However, if the same plan were devised to stop a murderer from pursuing a victim, it would be good. Keep this in mind.

Getting back to "good enough." There are times when a major goal needs to get done and a minor goal needs to be good enough. For example, if you're trying to win a stock car race and you pull into the pit, you may want your team to clear off the windshield while the tires are changed, but you may not have time for them to get every last smudge. If you wait for the mechanic to thoroughly clean it, you will lose the race, so good enough must be acceptable. When you stop a lower good at "good enough" in order to pursue a higher good, you are doing smart work. The purpose of cleaning the windshield is to have enough vision to win the race, not to win a spotless windshield contest. So, you meet your purpose. It's when you do the higher goods sloppily that you suffer, and so does your team. This may sound simple, but when you begin to reflect on this idea you will note that there are times when certain team players have fixated on the wrong things and have missed the point.

Goodness like this is possible only in light of truth, which is why I wrote about Prudence (second step is: know what is real, aka truth). Since goodness is the manifestation of something fulfilling the purpose of its creator's intention, you must ask what your intention is when you create. And you must make that intention known. If the mechanic cleaning the windshield is not made aware that the purpose is to win the race, then he will be frustrated when he can't complete his job. He will cause division and hold up the rest of the team. So, you need to make sure your entire team sees their role as part of the whole if you want goodness to permeate your organization. When you create a product, does it do what it is intended to do? When you establish an incentive program, does it really incentivize? When you have a meeting about your budget, does that meeting stay about the budget or is it side-tracked? When your team leaves a meeting, they sometimes say that it was a good meeting. What makes them say that? The answer is that it fulfilled its purpose.

Start with the basics: Is your product bad or is it good? What is its purpose, and is that being fulfilled? Are your opportunities for advancement a lie or genuine? Are you building something that, at the end of the day, makes the world better?

Knowing and doing what is good establishes a strong foundation because you become a purpose-driven organization. As your business scales, you need to renew your commitment to understanding your purpose. That perpetuates the commitment to do what's right—be it in terms of fair pay, safe work practices, or honest advertising—which will always win in the long term. It's not just what you do, it's how you do it that matters.

Incorporating the Transcendentals into business is not just about metrics or profit margins; it's about creating a legacy. A leader rooted in these principles doesn't only create a powerful business, but begins leading Giants—individuals who, irrespective of their roles, carry forward the values set forth, making impactful decisions aligned with unity, truth, beauty, and goodness.

BEAUTY

The Transcendental desire for beauty includes more than mere visual aesthetics. It is defined by Thomas Aquinas as "that which gives pleasure [delight] when seen." Although this definition suggests that it's limited to seeing, it is not meant to confine beauty to visual delight alone. Music, for example, is beautiful. Beauty has within it three parts: integrity, proportion, and clarity.

Beauty has integrity because it somehow presents completeness to its witness. You are not left lacking something about it when you experience it. A building half built is not as beautiful as it is when it is complete.

Beauty has proportion because it contains symmetry, harmony, and balance. We can't define this as much as we can feel it. A lack of these three makes most people uncomfortable to a mild or even strong degree.

Beauty has clarity because it has the power to impress or reveal a greater reality about a given thing. We know it when we see it, even when we aren't looking for it. When watching sports, commentators will quip when they see a great play, "That was a thing of beauty." In business, it refers to cultivating a pleasant, extraordinary experience for both employees and customers—e.g., a product that doesn't just function but brings customer satisfaction, a service that goes above and beyond, and an organizational culture that inspires. A beautiful culture is a harmonious culture. So, when building a business, prioritizing beauty uplifts how everyone experiences your company. As you scale, you'll increase your impact on families, communities, and even society, creating more beauty, whereas before there was simply a blank canvas.

The phrase that "beauty is in the eye of the beholder" is clearly based in reality because we all have particular tastes, but beauty is much more objective than subjective. Beauty is hardwired into us via natural law. For example, people universally say, "Wow, that is a beautiful sunset," and nobody says, "I hate sunsets. They're ugly." Beauty is innately perceived as good and true, which is why both men and women lower their guard when in the presence of a beautiful person. This demonstrates that goodness, truth, and beauty intermingle. On the other hand, we all recognize the absence of beauty, and we are less trusting of those things that lack beauty. The desire for beauty draws people to sit on a peaceful beach on a sunny day for relaxation, but a moist, dark cave or trash-filled city repels people. Beauty attracts us because we perceive it as good and, depending on the subject, trustworthy, whereas ugliness is perceived as bad.

The Call to Beauty Begets a Culture of Improvement

I recommend challenging your teams to make beauty part of the culture because beauty raises standards perpetually. Something is good when it is used for the purpose for which it is made and fills that potential. A paper cup is good when it is used to hold water, thus serving its purpose. The formula 2 plus 2 equals 4 is true, which is also complete. Even though we never tire of more truth or more goodness, they both can be complete. Beauty, however, is never complete. A cup can be more beautiful. It could be a crystal glass or a gold chalice. A gold chalice can then be more adorned with gems and on and on. This is why beauty is central to motivating higher standards.

Challenge your team to make all they do a "thing of beauty." As simple as that may sound, this will impact objective results. You will be surprised by what they do with it. Take meetings again as an example. A meeting is good if it does what it is supposed to do. You hold a meeting to come up with a marketing plan and you complete that goal. Therefore, it is good and it might have been beautiful. However, it could be more beautiful. It may have been stalled, delayed, sloppy, short of important details, and filled with irrelevant disagreements. If it meets its intended purpose, it's still good. But can it be more beautiful? Yes, it can be more organized. The materials could be better designed. The room could be more aesthetically pleasing. The conversation could flow better with more harmony, therefore creating an even better outcome.

Say this to your team and watch what they do. "That was a good meeting, but how can we make it more a thing of beauty next time?" If you take this seriously, marketing, concepts, accounting systems, and sales presentations will improve because we are all inclined to want more beauty, so your request will fall on fertile soil. A higher level of energy will spring up and a culture of "better" will ensue. This happens because we never tire of beauty and want more of it. So, if you center its importance by routinely saying things like, "This is a thing of beauty," or "Let's make this more beautiful," they will engage.

The beauty of a great idea carries tremendous weight. The beauty of a team working cohesively together in a respectful manner is inspiring. Invite beauty and praise it if you want more. Additionally, keep in mind that beauty is known to spark creativity and reduce stress.[2] This is exemplified in nature, where benefits such as clearer thinking and reduced stress are prevalent. Making your work environment as beautiful as possible is a catalyst for cultural beauty and creativity. It clears much of the path for your ability to influence.

HOW DO THE CARDINAL VIRTUES AND THE TRANSCENDENTAL DESIRES EMPOWER YOU TO ANSWER THE FOUR ESSENTIAL ORGANIZATIONAL QUESTIONS?

Let's return to the four essential organizational questions.

1. For what purpose was this made (the company, the product, the service, the meeting agenda, etc)?
2. What priorities should we focus on?
3. How will we go about it (broken down by tasks, timelines, and people)?
4. What will we do to stay on pace, finish on time, and measure our progress (aka know that we competed the goal)?

If you fail to ask a question, it can't be answered. If you and your team have either not asked these questions or not answered them properly or effectively, the root cause is usually coming from a deficit in the Cardinal Virtues or the application of the Transcendental Desires. The answer to each of the four questions leads to many other additional questions underlying the main answer. I will explain this more in the coming paragraphs. These are the first place to look to align your team and to increase productivity. Anything that comes before that is a Band-Aid. Buying a new back-office program or CRM when the Cardinal Virtues and Transcendental Desires lack is a fool's errand.

While all of the Cardinal Virtues and Transcendental Desires are used to empower answers to each question, some are more useful than others. I will highlight which Cardinal Virtues and Transcendental Desires enable the most effective answers.

1. For What Purpose Was This Made (the Company, the Product, the Service, the Meeting Agenda, etc.)?

Key Cardinal Virtues and Transcendental Desires Used to Empower the Answer: *Prudence, Goodness, and Truth*

In order to answer the first question, "For what purpose was this made?" you must employ the first three steps to Prudence. The first step for finding Prudence is tied to "For what purpose was this made?" because you must desire the outcome of that purpose. For example, let's use a professional football team. For what purpose was it made? The answer is simple: to win the Super Bowl. Considering that, this is how the three steps to Prudence supply you with what you need to answer the first of the four organizational questions in a meaningful way.

1. *What do we need to desire?*
   Win the Super Bowl.
2. *What is real about our situation regarding winning the Super Bowl?*
   Our quarterback is underperforming.
   We need a new stadium.
   Our defense has talent but needs a better coach.

3. *What do we need to do to do what is good?*
   Find a new quarterback.
   Find or build a new stadium.
   Get a new coach.

When you answer the question "For what purpose was this made?" you are giving a reason for the existence of a thing. This is the main reason all things are done within your organization. If you are a pro football team, as I said, the purpose is to win the Super Bowl. You may have a close second objective, such as to make a higher profit, but the closer you come to winning the Super Bowl, the more that outcome manifests. They are tied together. Of course, there are all sorts of other "goods" that can come from that purpose. Other examples would be stability for families who are employed by the team, the enjoyment of the fans while attending the games, the forming of character in the players, and the exposure of brands to a buying audience. But the main purpose is to win games. Every action and activity done by anyone associated with the team must be done to aid in the mission to win the Super Bowl. You don't run plays and practice so you can provide an opportunity to sell concessions. You sell concessions so you can attract fans who cheer on the team to give them a home field advantage to win the Super Bowl. You don't recruit players so you can employ talent scouts either. You recruit players to win the Super Bowl. You employ talent scouts to find the players to win the Super Bowl. So, when you need to solve any problem, make sure that you and your team know how everyone works toward that goal. This extends all the way to the custodial team who cleans the facility so the fans can cheer the team in a positive environment, therefore giving the home team an emotional advantage—to eventually win the Super Bowl. The three steps to Prudence are a big-picture view that illuminates the reason the organization was created, and they include a call to action to fulfill that purpose.

2. What Priority Should We Focus On?

Key Cardinal Virtues and Transcendental Desires Used to Empower the Answer: *Prudence and Goodness*

The process of establishing priorities is done by filtering the "good enough" from the "higher good." If you need a new stadium and a new quarterback, finding a good quarterback takes precedence. If you can do both, great, but if you can't, then get the quarterback. If you invest there, you will win games, therefore having more fans and revenue to get support to build the stadium.

When people get this wrong, it is usually summarized by someone saying, "They missed the entire point." Or "they treated a symptom but not the main problem." If you want these complaints to go away, get this second question right. This question is primarily answered with Prudence and truth, but goodness is at the core. Prudence because the three questions that make up Prudence are essential here. Truth because your emotions, bias, and ego can distract focus. Goodness is the focus here because when something is good, it meets its intended purpose. This helps determine when "good enough" works to fulfill the need (aka the dirty windshield of the race car driver) or perfect is required. When you move past a "good enough" issue to fulfill a greater priority, you pass the test of goodness. When you fixate on a low priority, raising its significance above a primary responsibility, you never get the "thing" that was created to manifest its purpose. It's the classic scenario described by "we got sidetracked in the meeting." I have more later on this point in chapter 9, covering the Four Daily Habits of Giants (keeping primary responsibilities primary). The key sub-questions to ask to identify priorities are:

1. *How does this activity (working a job, spending money, expending energy) fit into the big picture and bring us to our goal?* If you can't answer that question, you should abandon it altogether. Real-life

examples I have witnessed are unnecessary meetings or incentive plans that are not effectively aligned with motives to reach desired outcomes.

2. *Is it necessary?* If you can't connect the activity to the big picture, you can usually get rid of it. Getting rid of all wasted time, energy, and resources is key to driving growth and expanding your influence. I often see this when it comes to reporting. Data is important, but too much irrelevant data sent to high-level executives bogs them down in wasteful analysis. Getting data that matters or is summarized is necessary while data noise must be eliminated.

3. *Is there a better way?* If you can connect the activity to the end goal but it is inefficient or imperfect at moving you closer to that goal, you need to innovate or iterate improvements. This is the largest portion of activities, which include every role and process in the company from manufacturing to customer service.

4. *Is it "good enough" or does it need to be perfect to reach the ultimate goal?* If you can connect the activity to the end goal and it is essential, then you need to ask: Should we spend more on it, develop it further, or just go with it as is because other activities have priority? A practical example would be changing a company logo. At times this may be essential, such as when recovering from brand damage, but for the most part, the timing of such a thing is optional and potentially distracting to the highest-priority outcome.

These sub-questions within the main second question regarding priorities must be answered to move on to question three.

3. How Will We Go About It (Broken Down by Tasks, Timelines, and People)?

Key Cardinal Virtues and Transcendental Desires Used to Empower the Answer: *Beauty and Unity*

Once you have your "why" and then you have your "good enough" and "higher priorities" worked out, you must develop a plan of action. Unity is easy to understand here because the more you work as a team to accomplish the plan of action, the better the plan will be. Beauty assists in a more complex way. A great plan is only made possible by asking more penetrating questions. The most important questions you ask during this phase are creative questions. Creativity is a product of beauty. When the right answers are found, you will likely feel a sense of peace about the plan because it will be "a thing of beauty." Beauty has three parts, and they are essential here:

1. *Does the plan have integrity?*
   Is it complete? What is missing in this plan?
2. *Does the plan have proportion?*
   Is it balanced, symmetrical, and harmonious? These questions hit at the core of culture.
3. *Does it have clarity?*
   Do you understand it, and will its completion lead to a better place?

These questions form the best answers to the question "How will we go about it?" The added benefit is that they build the habit of improvement because, when we experience beauty, it opens our minds to what more beauty would be like, setting us on the path to finding it.

This surprises many people, but when you decide to make every task, every role, and every timeline a thing of beauty, you raise the bar by accelerating creativity. This is what gives culture fuel.

Interestingly enough, this "how" question requires the answer to all of the five "w's."

- Who? (Who will take responsibility for the task?)
- What? (Is the task defined shaped by all three parts of beauty: integrity, proportion, and clarity?)
- When? (What are the timelines and markers along the way? This is the building block for the next question.)
- Where? (What are the logistics?)
- Why? (There will be many lower "whys" tied to the higher "why," such as, in the previous example, winning the Super Bowl.)
- How? (What's missing on how this is executed?)

The plan should include the desired outcomes, the people involved, and the timelines. Who is responsible for accomplishing what task by when and how do they fit into the whole plan? How do they lead us to our "reason for existing"? Answering this question sets up the fourth essential organizational question.

4. What Will We Do to Stay on Pace, Finish on Time, and Measure Our Progress?

Key Cardinal Virtues and Transcendental Desires Used to Empower the Answer: *Fortitude, Temperance, Unity, Truth, Goodness, and Beauty*

The fourth question is all about execution. Staying on pace requires:

- **Fortitude**, which will keep you in the fight when things are stressful and arduous.
- **Temperance**, which will prevent you from trying to release stress in the wrong ways (something that has sidelined far too many people).

- **Unity**, which will be crucial to keeping everyone rowing in the same direction.
- **Truth**, which will be your marker for honestly interpreting data and facing the reality of the progress or lack thereof.
- **Goodness**, which will determine if you have completed the task.
- **Beauty**, which will raise standards as you move forward.

There are three main sub-questions to ask to get to the heart of this fourth essential organizational question:

1. *Are the timelines realistic (well-paced or either too slow or too fast)?* If the timelines are not challenging but possible, the motivation will go wayward. Striking the right chord is important.
2. *What is the method we will use to measure the progress?* This usually involves the implementation of a new technology or tracking system.
3. *Who is responsible for recognizing deficits or advanced progress and making those in command aware?* If you tax your leaders with too much analysis, they mix disciplines. Leading Giants is not about being an analyst. It is about influencing your team with the data once it is analyzed. Having an analytical mind is useful, but even when you have it, you're better off spending time influencing rather than analyzing.

Ultimately, you will know when you have obtained the goal by answering: Did the idea, job, project, or team fulfill the intended purpose of its maker? If so, well done, it was *good*.

GIANT TAKEAWAYS

Becoming a Leader of Giants and a transformer of nanos, who lives and leads by the Transcendental principles of unity, truth, beauty, and goodness, is inherently an internal process. You're wise to rarely, if ever, say these things out loud, but instead, do your best to live your own life in alignment with what is good, true, and beautiful. With that in mind, here are the best ideals to base your life and leadership on:

- **Unity:** Cohesion and alignment, first and foremost within yourself, and then infused into the organization you lead. Leading a united organization is more than just maintaining an image. It's about ensuring that every employee, from top leadership to the new hires, aligns with the core mission.

- **Truth:** The correspondence or agreement between a statement or belief and actual reality. The pursuit of truth is the greatest sign of strength. The denial of truth is the greatest sign of weakness. If you don't desire and embrace the truth, you are weak.

- **Beauty:** Hardwired into us via natural law, beauty is innately perceived as good and true. When building a business, prioritizing beauty uplifts how everyone experiences your company.

- **Goodness:** The foundation of ethics and moral principles, goodness should be the driving motivation to start a business. As the business scales, the commitment to doing what's right is what will *always* win in the long term. It's not just what you do, it's how you do it that matters.

Many people say they want success when really what they mean is they want the fruits of success. As shown, a great way to succeed is to incorporate the Transcendentals into your business. But it's not just about getting great metrics or huge profit margins; it's about creating a legacy. A successful and united business or organization that is based on what's good, true, and beautiful ensures the legacy you leave will uplift and inspire. Attaining your goals through commendable means makes the fruits of your labor even sweeter, and by doing so, you "transcend" the common struggles and sufferings inherent to our human experience.

6

Recruit the Best People—
If You Do This, You Will End
Up Diverse and United

FINDING AND HIRING GIANTS

If you want to build a team of Giants, you have to start by first being a Giant. Greatness attracts greatness. This, more than anything, primes you to find and attract the best people. Or, when you need to transform a team of ordinary people into extraordinary employees, you have to look for the best within them, leading them to become their best selves.

So, how do you find the best people and create a united organization? You could take one approach that, unfortunately, nearly every company in America tries: diversity, equity, and inclusion (DEI) standards. Or you could do what works instead. Now, if your goal is to divide your company, cause strife, and make people doubt themselves and each other, I say go ahead with the diversity programs. If you want a trusting, healthy organization with a resilient culture, I have a different suggestion that will satisfy any desire for diversity without compromising unity and success.

The idea that forced diversity programs fail is not new. The topic has been studied for nearly a century, but even more intensely for the past 40 years. One of the greatest summaries on the research was published in the *Harvard Business Review* in 2016 in Frank Dobbin and Alexandra Kalev's article "Why Diversity Programs Fail and What Works Better."[1] They state that "in analyzing three decades' worth of data from more than 800 U.S. firms and interviewing hundreds of line managers and executives at length, we've seen that companies get better results when they ease up on the control tactics." They explain, "Some of the most effective solutions aren't even designed with diversity in mind," and then continue:

> A good question to ask is: Do people who undergo DEI training usually shed their biases? Researchers have been examining that question since before World War II, shown through nearly one thousand studies. It turns out, that while people are easily taught to respond correctly to a questionnaire about bias, they soon forget the right answers. The positive effects of diversity training rarely last beyond a day or two, and the negative consequences are proven to not be worth it. A number of studies suggest that DEI trainings actually activate bias or spark a backlash. Nonetheless, nearly half of midsize companies use them, as do nearly all of the *Fortune 500*.

The data is so extensive and objective that it's hard to see how anyone promoting DEI doesn't know better. In the past several years, the aggressiveness of these ideologies has become so intense that reverse discrimination is silently depleting morale. It is silent because there is a huge persecution for people who don't toe the line of woke thinking. So then, why do so many businesses continue to do what fails? The answer is a lack of virtue fueled by fear. They do what they feel (not think) they're supposed to do according to people who have an agenda, and because they lack Prudence and Justice, they trade reality for a lie. To lead like a Giant, you need to reject adding programs that you know are offensive, unjust, and untrue.

Not every large company CEO has caved to the woke agenda. Elon Musk, the most successful entrepreneur in history, recently said, "I think DEI is very extremely anti-Semitic at its core and it's just generally anti-meritocratic, which I think is very dangerous. You want to have a society where you succeed based on your skills and hard work, and that's it. And it doesn't matter about your race, gender, creed, religion, nothing. You know? Just, are you good at your job? Do you work hard? Do you have integrity? Nothing more."[2]

In my company orientations, I'd often ask people to look around the room and tell me what they saw. People would consistently say, "It is a diverse group," to which I'd say, "Yes, it is. Do you know why? It's because we don't focus on diversity. We focus on one thing: that is to find the best people for the role. We know that you are the best and so is the person sitting next to you. That is the only reason you're here." Immediately, you could feel the room exhale relief and inhale a collective breath of confidence. If you want to find the most qualified candidates, and you don't discriminate, you will find them everywhere. If you take that approach and you don't end up diverse, it's not because of discrimination, it's because some people don't want certain jobs and you can't make them want those jobs just because you have diversity goals. It's that simple. Just seek out the best people—those who are the most qualified in a nondiscriminatory manner—and in all probability, you will end up with a diverse company. Focus on greatness, and the Giants will come running.

---

*To find the best people, hire first based
on virtue, then aptitude, experience, and
skill set, and, last of all, temperament.*

SUREFIRE WAYS TO HIRE

So, how do you find the best? The first thing to do is counterintuitive in many companies. That is to hire first based on virtue, then aptitude, experience, and skill set, and, last of all, temperament. When that is your approach, you will attract the people with the greatest potential and as a by-product you will build a more unified team. No one will question if they are there just to meet the company's quota. DEI just makes people defensive and emotionally unstable, and erodes culture. If there are any other reasons for employment, everyone doubts everyone.

When you hire someone because they're the best, there is clarity about what's expected of them. Hiring based on anything else, including nepotism, forced diversity, or the like, will instigate a cancer that erodes organizational culture. So, once you've attracted a recruit that has the signs of a soon-to-be-Giant, such as virtue, aptitude, and experience, these four steps will yield a diverse, united, and productive organization with an exceptional culture:

1. Hire Based on Virtue First

If you want to find and lead Giants, hire based on your best perception of virtue. This is not easy, and it's definitely not foolproof, but having virtue at the forefront is worth it. Hiring based on personality by using Myers–Briggs and other personality tests, despite great effort, fails to measure "earned" virtue and "succumbed" vice. Every temperament includes natural virtue and natural vice, which I will expand on later in the chapter. Suffice to say, choleric types are naturally driven but might mow you down to get their way. So, a personality test will reveal these inclinations that are present from someone's earliest years but will not reveal if that person has personally grown in virtue. A choleric who has "earned virtue," via hard work, will increase drive even more than he is naturally inclined. He will simultaneously tame his desire to mow someone down. Likewise, if he succumbs to his natural tendency toward vice, he will act like a dictator, caring almost nothing about those in his way. The good news is the more experience you have, the more you will hone your instincts to better identify virtue and vice early on. Until then, pay attention to inconsistencies and body language. Squirminess and gulping when retelling a different version of a story once you press for details may be a sign of dishonesty. Ask questions like, "Can you tell me a situation where you sacrificed something for someone else?" If the candidate has genuine examples of sacrifice, it will be a strong indicator of virtue. Also ask, "Are most people in your life supportive of you, or have you risen above a lack of support?" This question is effective because there is no right or wrong answer for them to guess at. Whether they have been supported or not won't determine your opinion. It will be more about how they answer that will give you insights. All types of answers could tip you off to a victim mentality or a strong will.

Nowadays, AI shoulders some of the workload of hiring candidates. A series of video interviews with AI measuring facial expressions to determine honesty and examine word choices can give insight into both aptitude and skill sets. This is valuable, but those programs are subject to human error once the data is in the hands of a person to make a final determination. Tools, tests, and techniques aside, virtue is best observed once a candidate is fully functional in their role. Thankfully, the more experience you gain when hiring and leading, the faster you will recognize patterns that lead to vice or virtue.

2. Consider Aptitude Second

Aptitude is the inherent ability to learn. If your company is dynamic, the roles of your people will evolve. Therefore, candidates need to have aptitude more than set skills or certain talents. The layered approach of seeking a candidate of high virtue followed by aptitude provides you the best, most flexible candidates that can grow within the organization. When people say that companies must be flexible, adaptable, and willing to grow, they're really talking about the people who run them.

The key to identifying a candidate with aptitude is to ask questions directly related to problem-solving. Gen Z, to their credit, is willing to learn many things outside of formal education. They are the first generation of learners who, from birth, can look up "how to" videos on YouTube, learning to do countless things. Older generations are often subject to historical thinking about problem-solving such as a formal class with a credentialed expert teaching it. That takes time and resources, barring many people from becoming highly integrated into micro-learning. Micro-learning is the quality adaptation of a new idea or skill that's applied via a short lesson. It applies to simple things like installing a dishwasher or fixing a technical issue with a camera. It clearly has limits, as none of us would want a person performing heart surgery after watching a few short, unaccredited YouTube videos, but it is a great indicator of aptitude.

Rapid learning of new skills and topics points to aptitude for learning other new things like being in a dynamic role with changing responsibilities for a growing company. A good question to ask is, "What have you learned lately?" Dive in more with, "Have you recently learned anything online for a home project or hobby, or taken a major course?" That question is usually enough to inspire a natural conversation that reveals the candidate's aptitude.

3. Next, Determine Experience and Skill Set

Many graduates don't work in the same field as their major.[3] This fact speaks to the prioritization of virtue and aptitude ahead of education, particular professional experiences, or degrees. Clearly, there are jobs that require specific degrees such as law, medicine, and finance, but even those positions are best filled with people of high virtue and aptitude. People often feign virtue, also known as virtue signaling, but when someone has it, it's unmistakable. Also, experience and skill sets can be lied about, like Mike Ross faking a Harvard law degree in the popular TV series *Suits*. It may land someone a job, but virtue is what leads someone to winning or losing in the long run, not skill sets or job experience.

So, when you're considering someone for employment, measure their experience and education against their virtues and aptitude. If a person has stayed stagnant but has a brilliant education, it may not be loyalty that kept them there. It might be a lack of understanding, weakness, or apathy—these kinds of things will only be revealed when you question their virtues and aptitude.

4. Finally, Consider Their Temperament

Knowing someone's personality and temperament allows you to place them in positions where they will thrive and uplift those around them. So, the last step is to evaluate if their temperament will be a good fit for their specific role and that position's broader reach in the organization. Will this person guard the organizational culture, or will they only look out for themselves?

Hippocrates, a Greek physician who lived from 460–377 BC, put forward the idea of four fundamental temperaments. These are choleric, sanguine, melancholic, and phlegmatic. Your temperament is the one you were born with. If you have, by way of virtue, trained yourself to behave better than your natural tendency from birth, that does not mean your temperament changed. It just means you have discipline. So, look at temperament from the perspective of your childhood.

- **Choleric**: Exhibits extroversion, quick thinking, decisiveness, self-confidence, and a strong drive to achieve results. Often visionary and goal-oriented.
- **Sanguine**: Characterized by sociability, enthusiasm, optimism, spontaneity, and liveliness. Sanguines are charismatic and adaptable communicators.
- **Melancholic**: Displays analytical thinking, detail orientation, organization, sensitivity, and depth. Melancholics are reliable, creative, and reflective individuals.
- **Phlegmatic**: Possesses calmness, easygoing nature, diplomatic skills, patience, and empathy. Phlegmatics are balanced, good listeners, and adaptable individuals.[4]

There are 16 different combinations of those four when blended. Each one of our temperaments, and many personality tests, are based on them. Every temperament has a natural virtue and an inherent vice. Cholerics, for example, are results-oriented, motivated, good leaders, visionary, are keen to resolve injustices, and they don't waste time. As mentioned earlier, left unregulated, the vices of a choleric include that they'll mow people over to get their way. So, to be a good choleric, you need "earned" virtues to amplify your base temperament and to tame down the vices you're prone to so you don't succumb to them. When using the four temperaments as a gauge for hiring, instead of seeing only the risk of negative behavior, make sure you're looking at the natural virtues as well.

I recommend doing some research to see how these four temperaments comprehensively work together. You can use them to identify strong fits for your organization and to place people in positions that match their natural strengths. To wet your whistle on your own further research, a brief look at a few temperament examples may be intriguing. When I was younger, occasionally I was impressed by sanguine people who had charisma and professional manners. Sanguine people can impress with proper attire, strong handshakes, and clever words. But if they have high levels of vice, they may convince you that they're going to be great at the job, without the actual intention to follow through. Experience taught me that many were only masters of that initial meeting. While many succeeded, several talked a big game but quit right away. Others stayed on but failed to live up to their self-billing. Some came to work just to take home a paycheck, but they were mentally checked out before they even started.

While sanguine personalities are people-oriented and do very well in interviews, they quit tasks quickly if they lack the virtue of Fortitude. With Fortitude, however, they can be very motivated to follow through. A choleric personality can also do well in an interview, but they are off-putting at times because they may seem overconfident. They will oftentimes outperform a sanguine if in an identical position because of their drive, but if they lack virtue, they will eventually burn bridges and have difficulty sustaining success. As shown, each temperament has a virtue and a vice, and it's your role to support people in diminishing vice and kindling their virtues. I encourage you to read additional books on the matter of temperament.

FIRST IMPRESSIONS MATTER

As I mentioned, AI is taking on a more significant role in hiring. This creates opportunities for efficiency, but they come with risk. Nobody will ever say, "What I loved about working there was having no contact with humans. My boss was a wonderful machine, whom I admired and respected." If too much of the onboarding process is done in an automated fashion, candidates may unconsciously determine that the leaders at the company lack confidence. They might also perceive that they don't care about people or unconsciously see themselves as subordinate to machines. It will set the stage for an impersonal, non-team-oriented, and uncollaborative setting. So, be sure people feel cared for early on if you want them to be cared for later in the process. They will reciprocate either your warmth or your coldness, determining the health and vitality of the culture.

In interviews, set the tone for the culture immediately.

Pay attention to the questions you ask in an interview because they set the tone for the upcoming culture. Questions like, "What's your five-year plan?" have been around for decades but yield almost no actual insights. Very few people have five-year plans and those who do normally don't act on them anyway. Most often these types of questions are asked to establish a feeling of superiority over candidates in a hypocritical way. It's hypocritical because the interviewer himself almost never has a five-year plan and clearly knows the interviewee doesn't have one either. Likewise, asking, "What's your greatest weakness?" is also fruitless. Who's really going to tell you their greatest weakness? No candidate will say, "I get drunk on the weekends and make poor choices," or "I'm addicted to porn, so I suffer in relationships." Instead, that same person is going to say, "I'm a bit of a perfectionist, but I've learned to manage it, and I have actually turned it into a superpower," or he'll say, "Sometimes, my standards are too high." The candidate and interviewer are both keen to the reality that none of this is true. In other words, they both know they are either lying or buying a lie. So, in the end, the interview process is little more than a power trip bolstered by placating lies. Hmm? And people wonder why their entire work experience at that company continues to feel the same.

The best candidates will sense insincerity during interviews. This is repelling because strength attracts. A great candidate has two things they need to satisfy before the smaller details are sorted through. He needs to know that the company and its employees are strong and that his potential value is noticed. Keep those simple goals in mind when you want the top talent on your team. To get to know the candidate better, I recommend you simply say, "Tell me more about yourself," regarding both general and specific topics. In addition to any necessary testing or supporting technology, this open dialogue is the best supplement to AI or other aptitude tests because it lets you understand what is important to the candidate in a natural manner. When you let him or her take over the direction of the conversation, you learn way more than you do by guiding it alone.

Another hiring pitfall that I have mentioned but I need to repeat because it is so common is that people often focus too much on resumes and qualifications. Sure, if I'm hiring a CFO, they absolutely must know accounting, strategy, and related laws. Without the necessary skills, their virtues are irrelevant. Yet once the basic qualifications are accounted for, I remind you that virtue becomes the core determining factor for potential employment. I've seen many aspiring candidates flaunt their business school credentials, but when it comes to certain roles like sales, their education means nothing. Complete novices outperform highly educated and seasoned professionals simply because they possess greater virtue and aptitude. They show up eager to learn and do the work.

If someone has the needed qualifications, is high in virtue and technical knowledge, and possesses an appropriate temperament, they're the gold standard. However, it's not about choosing virtue over experience or vice versa. It's about balance. I'd rather choose someone slightly less qualified but with more virtue because they will quickly catch up and often surpass those with more qualifications but less virtue. On the other hand, candidates with great resumes but who lack virtue tend to erode personally. If they are in leadership roles, they cause a decline for the people they lead. Whoever interviews candidates first will set the cultural tone for your new team members, so choose a person who exemplifies what you want duplicated.

MAKING IT REAL

By cultivating what is good, true, and beautiful you'll end up achieving the optimal goals of unity, profit, productivity, peace in the workplace, and all other signifiers of success. People will love coming to work, not because of grandiose ideals but for the profound simplicity that they feel good at work. People want to work with those who are committed, loyal, and compassionate, knowing that leadership has their back. When people love where they work and what they do, they'll seek out creative ways to succeed. But if there's one thing you can count on, it's that human nature will always tend toward lower standards without strong leaders pulling people back up to higher things. This takes daily work and focus because some people will cut corners and take advantage of their position despite a great culture. To mitigate this, if you start building a deep bench, starting today, you'll feel confident in those whom you attract, develop, and launch into higher levels of success.

GIANT TAKEAWAYS

- To create a united and diverse organization, focus on one thing: finding the best person for the role.
- To attract the best people, instill the Cardinal Virtues and the Aristotelian Transcendentals into yourself and your organization. Greatness attracts greatness.

- To hire the best people, do so first based on virtue, then aptitude, experience, and skill set, and, last of all, temperament.
- Doing these things, you'll end up achieving the optimal goals of unity, profit, productivity, peace in the workplace, and all other signifiers of success. This is how you'll have no problems retaining the best people and launching them to higher levels of influence.

Ask yourself these questions, and write down your answers:

- What contemporary initiatives am I following along with that may be harming instead of helping?
- How am I being pulled toward lower standards?
- What am I doing, on a daily basis, to lift myself up into greatness?

7

Build a Deep Bench, Starting on Day One

THANKFULLY, YOU'RE REPLACEABLE

Your ability to develop a deep bench and competent successors will determine a large measure of your success as a leader. Unfortunately, some poor leaders feel threatened by talented up-and-comers. Others fall into the false belief that nobody could ever do the things they do as well as they do them. This is a result of pride, and pride kills business as it kills all things. To overcome this, I encourage executives to ask themselves, "If I were not available to do what I do, who would do it?" A common answer to this question is, "There's nobody here who can." Whether it's a startup or an established company, it's imperative to develop talent from day one. While this responsibility is fairly obvious, it is not always heeded. Time and time again, solopreneurs fall into the trap of saying, "Nobody can do what I do," which just gets them stuck, sometimes for decades, in the trap of never being able to leverage influence because their pride prevents them from delegating. They trade what should have been a life of freedom for a self-made prison. Their bars are made of pride and the key to unlocking the gate is humility.

Even in larger organizations, I have too often seen an opposition to replacing oneself. This leadership pitfall happens within every industry, from single-store managers to Fortune 500 CEOs. It's a strange phenomenon when leaders in established companies forget they got into their position by replacing someone else in the first place. The offshoot of having too much pride to replace yourself is that it usually promotes the development of weak-minded employees, minion-type followers, and nonthinking loyalists—the opposite of building a deep bench. Thinking you are irreplaceable is absurd. Everyone is replaceable. Ironically, the more a person tries to convince you that they're irreplaceable, the more likely the opposite is true.

Exhibiting the knowledge that you're replaceable is attractive to others because it requires humility. When team members sense that you know you can be replaced, a series of good things enters the culture. Humble leaders listen to the counsel of others, empower others, and do everything they can to promote subordinates into bigger roles. Keep in mind, your driving objective is to lead Giants. We all know a giant is a creature who needs a large place to roam, a big diet, and goals to conquer, so you must develop a Giant-friendly environment immediately.

Great people recognize their value and only want to stay in organizations where they know leaders truly see them.

When you hoard your responsibilities and cling to your role by blocking up-and-coming talent, they will know it's happening and leave for greener pastures. To build a business the right way, you must surround yourself with the best people. If you find yourself thinking that no one is capable of your job, then you have some serious self-inquiry to do, which I'll get into later in the chapter. Being replaceable doesn't mean that anyone could be capable of taking over your role immediately. It takes time to replace higher-level roles, which is why it is essential to build a deep bench, starting today. Then, as you scale your organization, you'll have several outstanding people to choose from.

DON'T STEAL FROM THE NEIGHBOR KID

To expand your influence and grow your business, you must:

- Avoid taking on responsibilities that are not yours.
- Not do minimum-wage or medium-level work unless it is absolutely necessary and short-lived.
- Not do jobs you're already paying someone else to do.
- Delegate things that can easily be done by someone else.

Remember this: the more you grow your company, the greater your *responsibility* will be but the lesser your *responsibilities* must be. You, along with everyone else, have only 24 hours in a day. The process of reducing responsibilities and increasing responsibility is the only thing that facilitates growth. It requires leading Giants who accept the responsibilities you once had, while continuing the same formula of delegating tasks as you gain more responsibility. Over time, they will lead their own team of Giants, and the process is repeated over and over again.

Entrust others with as many things as you possibly can. This allows you to free up the mental space for making bigger decisions. Be sure to prioritize delegating the things you especially don't like doing because you can always find someone who does like them. Additionally, because those are the things you're most likely to put off, they can create overall delays.

In my early 20s, I purchased my first home. One day, a colleague, 20 years my senior, asked me what I did over the weekend. Among other things, I mentioned that I mowed the lawn. His reply shocked me. "Shame on you!" he said.

"What do you mean, shame on me?" I quickly said back.

He responded, "I didn't think you're the kind of guy who would steal from the neighbor kid."

I was confused. "What are you talking about?"

"That's a great job for the neighbor kid who you can pay X amount of dollars, who'd be absolutely thrilled to mow your lawn. Then, you're free to be there with your family. Instead, you stole time from your family, and you stole money from the neighbor kid."

Clearly, it can be a good example for your own children to see that you maintain things, not to mention working outdoors can be therapeutic. So, his analysis was at least partially flawed, but his insight illuminated a valuable lesson that there are two sides to delegation. On one side, you give someone else the opportunity to do what you might be hoarding, and on the other side, you gain time that you can use for others (or other more important things). At that time, since I was working so hard to get my business off the ground, I saw the greater value of being with my family that was made possible by paying the neighbor kid to mow my lawn. This insight extends beyond helping somebody with a deficit in quality time spent with family. It extends into creating organizational growth. Who are you robbing opportunities from by stunting growth in their responsibility or role? Who are you robbing by giving your time to the wrong things? What important decisions are you *not* making because you are doing lesser tasks?

I've seen many CEOs hang on way past their effective prime, even when there's a worthy and deserving person who is just as capable and should take the helm. So often, leaders have the means to move on, yet they'll hog roles, tasks, and their position when others should get promoted and thrive. This can be motivated by pride because they want to keep power for as long as possible. It's clear that there are situations that make sense for CEOs to stay on even if they have deep benches of capable people. Circumstances such as family businesses, age, or allowing time for future plans to jell are legitimate reasons to stay, but not all the duties must remain while they stay. Empowering others with more authority is especially important when a leader stays in his or her role for extended periods.

STEWARDSHIP VS. OWNERSHIP

I often see new entrepreneurs, young and old, start companies with destructive motives, of which vanity is the most common. Vanity, in business, is the desire to build something for the purpose of gaining personal recognition and power. It's possible to build a company that way, but it is impossible to build a great company with that motive. Any successful business leads to favorable personal recognition for its founder, and a certain amount of power accompanies the success. However, creation for personal gain stands in stark contrast to building an organization from the perspective of good stewardship.

Good stewardship presumes that you are building something greater than yourself that will live beyond your time there. Put another way, it's building something with no end in mind. That seems to contradict Stephen Covey's second habit of highly effective people, which is to begin with the end in mind, but it's a paradox, not a contradiction. While one should begin with their own end in mind, they should build a business with no end in mind. This attracts and retains greater talent and also inspires people to take personal ownership.

So, back to the point. While recognition and power will inevitably be part of success, they should never be the driving motivators. A good steward is a protector. Protectors build things the right way, with a solid foundation, meaning that you should build your organization with *its* power in mind. The business must stand on its own merit, not your personality or charm. You can't build a great company with long-term success if the business has no value without you. If you fall into this trap of creating a cult of personality, you'll act more like an egotist than a good steward. Ego mentality speaks often about "my" company, "my" ideas, and "my" authority. Stewardship mentality suggests "our" company or "the" business, even unconsciously demonstrating that the organization is bigger than the founder and will live on to the benefit of others after he or she moves on.

This can be tricky when you have a credential or skill that the new business thrives on and is the reason you found success in the first place. Dale Chihuly, the famous glassblowing artisan, was in a serious car accident, followed by a bodysurfing injury. The culmination forced him to delegate his work to other artisans. He found tremendous success in delegation and built a substantial business as a result. The reason I highlight Chihuly is because the hardest things to delegate are the ones in which you personally excel. If an artist can delegate something so particular to his own taste, style, and skill, then so can you.

The vanity pitfall is why many one-man-show companies stay that way and then eventually die off. Most solopreneurs complain that they "just can't find good people these days." This is a self-limiting belief that has trapped countless entrepreneurs. Often, right next door, there are other great companies, sometimes in the same industry, with great people. Instead of recognizing the work that was done for the growing company to effectively recruit and delegate, they claim the other company just "happened to get all the good people." These weak-minded leaders quip, "If I had all those good people that my competitor has, I'd be just as successful." They fail to see that attracting great talent is one of the most important qualities and skills of great leaders. It doesn't happen on its own; it takes honesty and hard work.

They fail to ask, "What is it about me that makes it so I can't attract, train, retain, develop, and launch new people to greater levels?" In order to attract great talent and to lead Giants, you must own your past failures and current status to attract good people. If you don't own it, you will perpetuate it. Justifying bad circumstances only commits you to continue repeating your errors. The way out is self-examination and sitting coura-geously in the discomfort that it brings. What have you done to repel great talent? What do successful people do to attract the very best? The answers lie in two primary traits: strength and humility. Ironically, humility is the highest form of strength, which is why it is so attractive.

STRENGTH ATTRACTS: AN ESSENTIAL PRECURSOR TO BUILDING A DEEP BENCH

Words never said are, "I loved working for him because he was so weak, and I could push him around." Or "I loved how prideful he was." You become intensely attractive to the people you lead when you have the courage to say things like, "How can I help?" Or "I'm sorry. I was wrong. I made a mistake." Or "I like your idea better." In contrast, when you say, "That's your fault," "Your problems are not my problems," and the like, you are perceived as weak and distinctively prideful. As a result, nobody wants to follow you because you're not taking them where they want to go. Strength and humility are what drive your stewardship and expand your influence. They are what makes you develop better training pro-grams, clearer job descriptions, more reasonable policies, and so forth. They're also what prevents you from saying, "Nobody can do what I do," which is immature, silly, and small-minded.

To be an effective, respected leader, and a great steward of your com-pany, you must create an environment in which people know they can advance. To that, you might say, "Well, my organization isn't big enough to have room for advancement." If that's true, then you need to make it bigger. That is not a flippant statement. Make it bigger. If you have a great business that provides a great product or service, then why not grow it? You might say, "I want a small business. I want to have a local coffee shop and have a peaceful life, serve some coffee, interact with neighbors, and just have fun. I don't really care about growing it." I understand the allure and value of living a peaceful and simple life. However, I'm confident there's a better way and it doesn't compromise the peace and simplicity this type of person desires.

Consider that you might actually build a coffee shop that people really love, and the neighborhood starts to depend on it. You make it a place that they love to go, and now, since you decide you're done, you take that away from them. If this coffee shop is not just a self-indulgent thing, but actually something built for your customers, which is the essence of good business, then wouldn't you want to do something to allow it to live beyond you? When you build a business with the idea that it is bigger than you, and it is fundamentally for others, it entirely shifts the perspective. This is stewardship. This is the foundation of cultivating genuine, long-lasting influence.

The "it's done when I'm done" mentality is like renting a car. What do people say when they rent cars? "I'm going to drive the hell out of this thing! It's not mine, so I don't really care." Ironically, a "renter" attitude is more present with a vanity-based entrepreneur who doesn't see his business lasting longer than he does. The mentality of valuing the thing that you're building is a key differentiator between steward-ship and ownership, which is essential to embody and teach to everyone you lead to carry on beyond your stay. When you value something, what do you do with it? You maintain it. You take care of it. You show-case it. You talk and brag about it. You protect it. If your business is something you value, of course you're going to do all those things because you want it to last.

Second to establishing a virtue-based culture, building a deep bench is how to best protect your business. However, regardless of size or industry, leaders constantly miss that reality. Take Lee Iacocca, a well-known figure in the American automotive industry, celebrated for his role in the development of the Ford Mustang. He later moved to Chrysler where he led the company out of near bankruptcy in the early 1980s. During his time at Chrysler, Iacocca wrote books, appeared on the covers of magazines, and was known for his iconic cigar-smoking. He was, by any stretch of the imagination, an incredible leader—highly effective and sought after. Few people have or ever will accomplish more than he did. But as his popularity grew and he was out signing autographs, the company started to struggle. Despite Iacocca's incredible achievements, for a while, critics say, he didn't prepare an effective second line of leadership, which created a leadership vacuum. That's debatable, but if it's even on the radar of something he might have missed, it demonstrates that even the most effective thinkers and innovators can miss important yet basic concepts in leadership. Building a deep bench starting on day one is often on that list. If Lee Iacocca could miss this, even for a moment, then we should all guard against our own shortcomings.

HOW TO BUILD A DEEP BENCH

Weak-minded people sometimes worry that building a deep bench and having good people somehow threatens their own influence. A virtuous leader knows it's not a threat; it's essential to success. Having incredible, trustworthy people provides an opportunity to take vacations so you are more refreshed when you return. It gives you an opportunity to discover better ideas because you're not the only one coming up with them. It gives you the spaciousness to enjoy a particular lifestyle while delegating more things for the benefit of all. It also powerfully expands the scope of your business. Having a deep bench is essential if you want to be a leader of substance and accomplishment.

So, how do you do it?

1. **Attract** (recruit).
2. **Develop** (train and mentor).
3. **Launch** (promote).

As I've already covered how to hire Giants, in this section we will focus on developing and launching your successor. Once you've found the right person or people, you don't immediately say, "You're here to take over my role." You train and then test them. You give them, along with multiple other candidates, certain levels of responsibility. Intuitively, they will know that you are seeking to elevate one or more to higher roles, but it's not a good idea to start talking about it too much. This can result in people feeling pitted against each other or create contrived notions of preferential treatment. That can happen regardless. It's quite normal and is often a part of the process even if you don't instigate it. Simply observe them all, see how they're doing, and keep giving them a little bit more responsibility. There is tremendous value in being able to compare the quality of decision-making and actions of several candidates even if you have an intuition about one over the others.

When I develop my successors, I say, "I'm about to have a conversation, and I want you to listen in. Afterward, I'd like to discuss why I made the decision and get your thoughts." Doing this, I am able to understand their thinking processes, and they are able to understand mine. I help educate them where they lack experience, but I also benefit from their insights. The synergistic result accelerates their mentorship while simultaneously allowing us to make better decisions together immediately. When you mentor, you empower. This requires humility, good judgment, self-control, fairness, and bravery—essentially, the four Cardinal Virtues in action.

YOUR TOP 10 LIST

An exercise that will help you develop a deep bench is creating your Top 10 List. This is a list of the top 10 candidates who could succeed you in your role or who could fill other essential leadership roles as your organization expands. It is a list that is updated monthly based on performance, acumen, and, most importantly, virtue. A common challenge is that you may not think you have 10 solid candidates. Even if this is true, it's imperative to list them out even if none of them are seemingly qualified or talented. This exercise tells you a lot about who you attract and why. If you genuinely don't have talented people you can list, then there are foundational changes you need to make.

Here's the other reason I have people make the list: leaders often don't see the talent right in front of them. For many years, I have asked the leaders of my organizations to share their Top 10 List with me before I meet with their teams. Obviously, the list is confidential, but it allows me to see how well they identify talent. I am often pleasantly surprised by the depth of the talent and the ability of the leaders to recognize the best up-and-comers. Other times, I observe the leader not recognizing the top talent and selecting less-qualified people. This happens for two common reasons. First, if the leader lacks the wisdom, experience, and knowledge that come from Prudence and Justice. Having failed to work on themselves, they can't identify what they lack. Lacking experience makes them choose charismatic people without much to offer besides charisma. Charisma may get them placed high up on the list, but it won't get them far without virtue, acumen, and experience. The second reason that some leaders fail to provide a solid Top 10 List is because they feel threatened by the talent beneath them. This is easier to understand in politically driven organizations that don't use merit as much as they do shoulder rubbing and backstabbing. However, as common as this misguided notion is, leaders are not made smaller by the success of their teams; they are made bigger. Imagine the legendary Packers coach Vince Lombardi getting jealous of Bart Starr, the starting quarterback. That sort of contrived competition for credit would have destroyed the Packers' success and prevented them both from becoming the legends they are. Greatness begets greatness. So, be bold and list your top 10 so you know who to focus on as time moves forward.

The Top 10 List teaches you to recognize the strengths and deficits of the up-and-coming leaders, acting as a filtering and training tool. If a candidate lacks good judgment, they need to be trained. If a candidate won't improve even after being given proper training, they need to be replaced within the Top 10 List, and if it continues, within the company altogether. Knowing how to replace others gets you more in touch with how you're also replaceable. That can motivate you to improve while you choose to stay and know that there is someone out there who can take your role when you're ready to move on.

GIANT TAKEAWAYS

You, along with everyone else, have only 24 hours in a day. So, entrust others with as many things as you possibly can. This allows you to free up the mental space for making bigger decisions—aka the greater your *responsibility* will be and the lesser your *responsibilities* must be. This is the essence of leveraging your influence and leading Giants.

- Who are you robbing opportunities from, stunting growth in their responsibility or role?
- Who are you robbing by giving your time to the wrong things?
- What important decisions are you *not* making because you are doing lesser tasks?

How to Build a Deep Bench

1. **Attract** (recruit).
2. **Develop** (train and mentor).
3. **Launch** (promote).

In order to attract great talent and to lead Giants, you must own your past failures. If you don't own them, you will perpetuate mistakes. Justifying bad circumstances only commits you to continue repeating your errors. The way out is self-examination and sitting courageously in the discomfort that it brings. So, while you make your Top 10 List, ask yourself:

- What have I done to repel great talent?
- What do successful people do to attract the very best?

8

Mastering Leadership Does Not Always Require Overtime

t's commonly said that the Great Wall of China is the only man-made structure that is visible from space. This objectively false statement is perpetuated repeatedly by many despite being totally untrue. Why do people say and believe things like this? I suppose it makes them feel smart or maybe they just find it fascinating, so they want it to be true. Humans have the amazing ability to parrot untrue ideas. One prominent false idea that is repeated in business is that to be a great leader or employee, you must work long hours and succumb to the "grind." The impulse that working long hours will inevitably bring success affects all levels of leadership, across every industry. Law firms exhibit the best example of what not to do when it comes to leveraging time as a Giant. Due to the legal profession's billing model, a culture of long hours is not only expected but is the fundamental measure of one's value to a firm. The more time they invest, the higher their billing rate rises, which increases their contribution to the firm's profitability. Of course, they must also excel in legal proficiency and litigation abilities.

To build a great organization and lead effectively, you must completely dismantle the notion that employing or being a work-obsessed person will yield success. If you work eight hours and I work 16 hours, am I going to be twice as productive as you? Absolutely not. If it were true that more hours equals more success, then the best anyone can be is three times better than someone who works eight hours. The top CEOs in the world are not three times better than the average leader—they're 15,000 times better! Furthermore, an elite few have found ways to run multiple multibillion-dollar companies but with way less time than their contemporaries who run just one business. Some even make it home for dinner every night. Meanwhile, a naive leader will convince themselves that they need to stay in the office for long hours, even after everyone's left.

Personally, I find it curious when people brag about how many hours they work. Long hours are not necessarily a sign of hard work because many people work lazily. Working long, lazy hours is unimpressive because it lacks virtue. Working long hours in a non-lazy fashion is still unimpressive because it lacks savvy and efficiency. Business is about getting more done in a shorter period of time and with fewer resources, which is why great leaders think about results, not hours. Anyone can work longer. Ask yourself, why would a person brag about something that any capable human can do? In grade school, would you have bragged that an assignment most students completed in 20 minutes took you two hours? Would you brag about taking longer to run a race than everyone else? Clearly these are signs of a deficiency in qualification and ability. Yet, in the working world, people think it is impressive to talk about how long they work. It's not.

Leadership is about innovating and inspiring. It's about the vision you create, the culture you cultivate, and the people you empower. As a leader, my team and I have had to work extra hours from time to time to meet a deadline. There are times when this makes sense. However, many people who *regularly* stay in the office till late o'clock often do so to:

- Build self-esteem.
- Justify their income.
- Compensate for insecurity.
- Please someone else.
- Stay afloat due to an unreasonable workload and no authority to delegate.
- Hide from responsibilities they don't want to face outside of work.
- Prevent themselves from feeling the loneliness that awaits them when they leave work.

There are rare instances of a leader who's being "strategically imbalanced" with intense, devoted effort for a specific project or opportunity. Working two to four additional hours, for a short, strategic amount of time, can significantly move the needle. But finding others who can, should, and want to do that work is a way better strategy.

If you only use more hours to lead your teams and grow your business, you're limiting the entire organization's potential because time is a finite resource. To be a great leader and have an even better personal life, you must learn how to maximize your influence with fewer hours over time by mastering good decision-making, delegating effectively, and leveraging your resources. These are all attributes of the Cardinal Virtues and being able to practically enact positive moral principles.

Balancing your personal life with professional endeavors is something everyone must strive to do. Taking time for rest and reflection, rather than constant work, is essential to truly understanding and appreciating life. Finding purpose in your life beyond your job is important. On your deathbed, you won't say, "I wish I had spent more time in meetings." If you only use more hours and hard work to attain success, you're going to say, "I wish I was there for my kids." "I could have gone to that concert." "I should have upheld the family tradition of going camping every year." It's healthy to want to spend more time doing the right thing, for the right people, at the right time in life. But when you pour all of your hours into work, you will regret it at some point if it comes at the cost of more important things.

Exhaustive repetition mistaken as hard work will block you from attaining success.

Most people still assume that I work long hours. They say, "I know you're busy and you probably work seven days a week to grow like that," or "Thanks so much for taking this call. I know how busy you are." Thankfully, they are incorrect. I've found lasting success by implementing these three keys to exponentially multiplying my time, which you can also use to engage in far more important things:

1. Make better decisions.
2. Surround yourself with great people.
3. Leverage your resources.

These three things are the solution to scaling your organization and increasing freedom of time. With them, you will work fewer hours while getting more done. To be clear, working hard is commendable, but exhaustive hours mistaken as hard work will block you from attaining success. Once you begin making better decisions for yourself, you'll lead others with greater conviction and confidence. This means finding better-suited people or systems that can easily resolve any exhaustive tasks or repetitive responsibilities. This increases your responsibility, which allows you to make better decisions while simultaneously requiring you to trust others. By effectively leveraging your resources of time, money, networks, and technology, you'll see productivity and prosperity rise exponentially.

Make Better Decisions

One of the ways that you know you're in the presence of a person who practices Prudence is that they make decisions very quickly. That is to say, they make decisions as quickly as possible according to the topic, without wasting time. This only happens because of practice, meaning taking consistent action toward positive goals. If you're playing a sport or learning any new skill, there are many decisions you need to make to execute your goal, like when to pass the ball. An inexperienced person is going to make the decision too early or too late, therefore missing the opportunity. Over time, however, that same person will have compounding success, creating "muscles" of intellect, will, and memory. As these muscles develop, they will make quicker, more prudential decisions. This is not an easy process, but one that's required to be influential. The practice of making important decisions, like managing a family or business, requires devotion and discipline—two actions of being prudent. Your success will be determined by the weight of the good decisions you make versus the weight of the bad decisions.

You must also measure the weight of the issue with the speed of the decision. For example, the imprudent person takes 20 minutes to decide where to eat lunch when they only have a 30-minute break, and then another 15 deciding what to choose from the menu. This is acceptable if you're celebrating an anniversary, but not when you have to get back to work. Imprudent people will also swing the pendulum in the opposite direction and spontaneously buy a car, having given a big purchase very little consideration. Clearly, you can't claim to be prudent just by making quick decisions.

A litmus test for knowing if a decision was or will be prudential is asking yourself three questions. These will look familiar, as they are the first three steps to mastering a decision discussed in chapter 1:

- Did you desire what was morally, ethically, and strategically good for the situation and for all involved?
- Do you know the reality of the circumstance, without the influence of self-deceit?
- Did you act on what is good after you understood the circumstance?

If you can answer yes to all three questions, you will be fast and effective with your decision-making.

Decision-making in leadership relies on the rapid recognition of patterns. As leaders in any sector accumulate experience, they become adept at identifying patterns in behaviors, excuses, justifications, and thought processes. Similarities in human nature become evident, and while situations remain open to deviations, a great leader trusts past experiences to provide a road map for expected outcomes.

One of the things I admired while observing one of my successors was his exceptional decision-making. He took action, leading others quickly and accurately. When outsiders were visiting the organization, they could not believe how fast he made decisions. In their companies, things that would have taken a committee meeting, four hours of consultation, and 12 other people to concur, people in our organization did in a few seconds.

Surround Yourself with Great People

When you want to build something great, attracting extraordinary people is one of the most important skills you need as a leader. You can attract people with power, money, prestige, authority, a good title, or a great company reputation. But then, there comes a point where you need to retain them. Retention is a continuation of attraction by constantly elevating opportunity, authority, and/or satisfaction. But first, you need to know how to surround yourself with the best.

What is most attractive to great people is strength and significance. Great people want to be a part of something significant because they aren't looking for their work to give them an increased sense of self. Small-minded people are usually drawn to just one thing, like being "number one" or their job giving them their sense of identity. Therefore, small-minded people are easily attracted to ignorant ideas or even bad business practices. This is why some admire twisted honors such as how leaders never see their families due to the many hours they work or how they bend the truth to close deals.

Great people build long-lasting things that have deep meaning. There is a classic parable of three men working with bricks. A passerby asks the first man, "What are you doing?" to which he replies, "Laying bricks." The passerby approaches the second man and asks the same question, "What are you doing?" to which the second man replies, "Building a wall." Finally, the passerby asks the third man, "What are you doing?" to which he replies, "Building a cathedral to glorify God and bring awe and beauty to millions of pilgrims over the centuries." I have heard people basically interpret this parable with the notion that the first two men missed the entire point, and the third man is the one whose example you should follow. However, great people are like all three men combined. They enjoy the idea of winning the day; therefore, they break long projects down into smaller chunks. This provides them an opportunity to get the satisfaction of accomplishment along the way in each portion of the activity, from laying a single brick to building a wall to the grand idea of the cathedral.

Leverage Your Resources

This might sound oversimplified, but if you're doing something someone else can do, get them to do it. Remember, the larger you grow your organization, the bigger your responsibility will be but the fewer responsibilities you should have. (You can count on me repeating that over and over.) Delegating can be mentally and emotionally taxing, but eventually, it creates a juggernaut of organizational energy.

However, if you don't allow your team access to the best tools, technology, and information, delegation will fall short. Leveraging resources is easier than most people think. If you paint a clear vision, get good people in place, and lead them to use the available resources, then you don't need to be the one to do all the problem-solving and work. Trust your people to be the ones to use what they have available; just make sure there are incredible resources for them to use.

Leveraging all types of resources will assist in making you an effective leader. You might not believe you have assets to leverage, but I assure you, there is more available to you than you may think. Successful entrepreneurs figure out how to gain access to resources, yet they all do it a bit differently. Some people borrow money or get rounds of financing in order to hire good talent. Others find good talent on a part-time basis while building enough capital to bring them on full-time. Many companies use a combination of both. Similarly, some leaders build their own technology while others lease or subscribe to third-party resources. Either way, the technology is there and so are the people. When people fail to leverage resources, they usually buy into the lie that they don't have any access to them, or, unfortunately, they don't maximize what they already have. While your resources may not be the same as someone else's, use what you can, and use it effectively.

You may have noticed that these three keys are a summary of what you've read in the previous seven chapters. I've done this intentionally, especially because, as we dive deeper, we're moving out of the realm of ideals and into specific, practical strategies. That being said, your job is to inspire others to achieve more by working smarter rather than just working harder. This means recognizing and rewarding good results, as well as correcting inefficiency and attitudes that erode a great organizational culture. Ultimately, the path to exceptional leadership and a fulfilling personal life is not about increasing hours; it's about optimizing them.

RECREATION IS WHERE YOU RE-CREATE YOURSELF

When you take a break from work, the way you use that time matters. Recreation is where you should find inspiration, rest, and regeneration. It is not a time to exhaust yourself or mind-numbingly do things that produce no value in your life. That's not to say that watching a comedy or enjoying a TV series is bad, but it must be enjoyed in proper doses. If your activities re-create you, you'll have more energy as you enter back into work.

If you don't properly balance leisure and work, it can lead to dissatisfaction in both areas. If you avoid personal commitments by overworking, you'll be unfulfilled at home. When your leisure is misused, it can make your work feel overwhelming. These imbalances can lead to emotional numbness, preventing you from fully experiencing and appreciating your life. Josef Pieper, an important figure in the resurgence of Thomistic philosophy, wrote *Leisure, the Basis of Culture*.[1] First published in 1948, in it, Pieper suggests that the fundamental essence of being human isn't to work but to engage in leisurely activities. However, Pieper differentiates between the common understanding of leisure as idleness and leisure as a state of contemplation in which one can realize the higher things in life.

According to Pieper, and I agree, the Greek idea of *skole* is the true nature of leisure. This concept was tied to education, culture, and worship. For them, leisure was not just about relaxation, but about the pursuit of creativity, goodness, and beauty in one's life. Recreation, a crucial part of cultivating virtue, isn't laziness, but rather the active pursuit of wisdom and understanding. It is the ultimate goal of a well-lived life, reaching far beyond modern ideas of normalized escapism like entertainment, vacation, or indulgence.

Life can feel like a whirlwind of responsibilities, but never forget that at the heart of it all is your "why." The giggles of your child running to you after a long day, the comfort of a spouse's smile after an intense meeting, or the joy in your friend's eyes when you walk through their door. These moments and relationships are the treasures we often risk losing if we bury ourselves in work, pursuing success at a great cost.

Imagine a home without laughter, warm hugs, or shared memories. A place where time has become a resource hoarded for egotistical abuses of entrepreneurship. Picture loved ones waiting for a dinner that never happens, for a promised day out that constantly gets postponed, or an intimate conversation that always gets cut short by unsilenced notifications. Imagine children growing up with a vague memory of their parents' presence, a spouse sleeping alone in a cold bed, dreaming of warmth. It's a grim image known to millions of people—an echo of a life that could have been vibrant, filled with love and joy.

If you have been working long hours for imprudent reasons, know that it's never too late to change the story! Today can be the day you choose not to abandon, but to embrace the people and experiences that mean the most to you. This moment can be when you decide to stop making work your life and instead a means to a better life. If guilt is pulling at your conscience, don't let it anchor you in regret. Instead, allow it to propel you forward as you course-correct and find balance. Seize the day and seize it now.

GIANT TAKEAWAYS

This chapter is somewhat of a summary of the previous seven chapters. It is the start of moving you out of the realm of ideas and into specific, practical strategies. Your job is to inspire others to achieve more by working smarter rather than just working harder. This means recognizing and rewarding good results, as well as correcting inefficiency and attitudes that erode a great organizational culture. Ultimately, the path to exceptional leadership and a fulfilling personal life is not about increasing hours; it's about optimizing them. To do this, and to lay a strong foundation for your actions going forward, embrace the three key strategies to exponentially multiply your time:

1. Make better decisions.
2. Surround yourself with great people.
3. Leverage your resources.

Also, remember that when you take a break from work, the way you use that time matters. Recreation is where you should find inspiration, rest, and regeneration. It is not a time to exhaust yourself or mind-numbingly do things that produce no value in your life. Recreation, a crucial part of cultivating virtue, is the active pursuit of wisdom and understanding.

9

Four Daily Habits That Separate Giants from the Pack

DAILY HABIT 1: BRING YOUR THOUGHTS TO LIFE WITH ACTION

In chapter 12, I will discuss how a healthy organizational culture prevents problems. There, I dive into the cultural impacts of healthy sales. I will touch on the structural aspects of the axiom that "nothing happens in business until someone sells something." For now, we'll explore the obvious: when nothing is sold, nothing happens. Action is essential to accomplishing anything. Unfortunately, I've seen people plan, strategize, or procrastinate themselves, their team, or their company to death. Maybe not literally, but overthinking paralyzes progress. As Thomas Edison famously said, "Vision without execution is hallucination."

Many people sit on the couch with a beer and chips watching *Shark Tank* reruns while declaring, "That was my idea!" The difference between the couch potato and the people on the show is that the entrepreneur took action. Ideas are a dime a dozen, but people who execute are like 5-carat, clear diamonds: they're rare. Many people put in little effort past just thinking of something great. What they do best is take credit, overthink, and remain static. Often, these are the same people who do just enough to land a job, but they don't decide to be great at it.

Leading a business requires forethought and planning. However, most leaders can relate to the Mike Tyson quote, "Everyone has a plan until you get punched in the face." Overplanning doesn't always pay off because once you get started you will need to adapt to the metaphoric punches you take while executing. Taking action with the flexibility to pivot if necessary is better than planning for so long that opportunity passes. If you simply just take action, you'll see results. They may not always be positive results, but they will provide insight and the experience gained by execution will be valuable. When you talk to successful leaders, especially entrepreneurs, you'll hear something like, "At times we had no idea what we were doing; we just started doing something. Eventually, we'd see, 'Oh, that's not working. Let's change it over here and pivot this way.'" Businesses are founded on action, not on thought alone.

Billions of companies have been pondered in the minds of many, but few have been started and even fewer have been successful. At the core, the reason for this is a lack of understanding leadership. Transforming a concept from paper to reality requires effective leadership. From fundraising to recruiting, leadership drives results. The confusion about leadership stems from the poor example of many pseudo-leaders, like those who merely leverage financial resources as incentives to motivate others. Sales leaders do this by having never-ending contests. Other, more narcissistic leaders manipulate people with a cult of personality, fan following, or a certain level of intimidation. Others use advanced technology to wow minions. In the end, these techniques, alone, fail to attract and develop strong, independent-minded Giants who help them gain traction on a new idea. As such, the work you're doing to develop the Cardinal Virtues and Transcendentals will set you apart. It will show you how to lead in an authentic manner by taking prudent action and correcting mistakes as they happen.

DAILY HABIT 2: FIND CONCRETE REASONS TO BELIEVE

One of the biggest differences between a nano and a Giant is that the nano is always expecting someone else to build his or her convictions. Giants, on the other hand, find reasons to believe and they do it daily. "What's on my agenda today? Okay, here's how and why we can get that done." They set a goal and begin building a realistic case for how and why they can and should accomplish it. I was once asked about my views on discrimination, as though there should be anything other than one view, which is *don't do it*. To catch my interviewer off guard, I responded, "Actually, I've considered discriminating. I thought long and hard about it, but after further consideration, I have decided that I *will* work with MBAs." This not only brought humor to a potentially charged topic, but it highlighted an important point, which is that a resume may impress, but it doesn't guarantee results. In my organizations, we recruit the very best people and have discovered they have a common trait: they find reasons to believe in what they want to accomplish and have built their conviction to the degree that they often defy the odds. Of course, we required particular degrees related to specific roles such as finance and legal counsel, but beyond that, specific qualifications didn't matter to us. Case in point, one of the greatest software developers we had was a theologian. He taught himself software development on the side and was confident he could handle the job. We were hesitant, considering the formal training our other developers had. But he came with solid references and gave us reasons to believe in him. He turned out to be an absolute wizard. To this day, he is one of the best I've ever seen, and his work ethic and expertise made it easy to believe in him.

We made sure to not stunt our growth by overthinking someone's resume or credentials. Instead, we looked for Giants, and we found them in every corner. Consider how many entrepreneurs have become highly successful without degrees but with conviction. Ironically, many wouldn't even meet the minimum job qualifications in most companies. Yet they often go on to build a company even bigger than the one that would pass them by for not meeting their "standard." They are action oriented, knowing that's the only way to gain the experience needed to succeed. Qualifications can open doors, but action and expertise built through conviction keep you in the room.

Whimsical Belief Systems vs. Strong Reasons to Believe

One thing I've noticed about people with MBAs is that when I've hired them to lead new projects or divisions, they fail to instill belief in themselves and others. The reason is that they often craft detailed spreadsheets with appealing projections showing tremendous sales and profits but without articulating reasons to believe those results can come to life. Forget the spreadsheet; go hire someone and make a sale demonstrating to me that the idea you have is appealing to a real customer. Then build a spreadsheet scaling the already proven idea. It's astonishing how often highly educated people miss that projections are pointless without real action. I'd rather be presented with rough, even loss-making projections that demonstrate some kind of actionable plan. This gives something concrete to work on, to improve the numbers and refine an approach, because it shows there's actual momentum behind their ideas.

Don't get me wrong. I value good projections, data, all of that. But if I had to choose, I'd prefer someone who's action-oriented over someone who's just great at manipulating a spreadsheet. It's like a salesperson who's the least productive on the team but gives lofty projections at meetings. They might have only sold $100,000, a relatively small amount, while the top performer in the group sold $5 million. Yet they confidently project they'll hit $7 million in sales next year. This will make some people say, "Oh, great projections, Bob. You've made a great mental turnaround. You have really high goals; good for you—$7 million. That's great."

You and I both know Bob's not going to sell $7 million. Nothing about him says $7 million. What he wants is recognition without effort. This is vice-orientated behavior and only weak leaders affirm it by telling Bob they buy his projections. Instead, here's what Giants do. They pull Bob aside and say, "Hey, Bob. First of all, yes, accolades on big thinking. But what's causing the difference in attitude? What are you actually going to do to make $7 million a reality? We need a little bit more here in terms of your action plan. When January hits, tell me more about the activities you will be doing on a day-to-day basis and why/how that will increase your sales from this year."

I often asked division heads in revenue-generating departments for a **Reasons Document**. In essence, this is a document that satisfies the question: *Why should I, we, you, or anyone believe your goals/plans are going to become reality?* It should include objective calculations such as directly increased and measurable productivity. It also includes subjective analysis such as how and why attitudes have changed. So, when department heads report their numbers, we always ask for convincing reasons such as, "How and why will the projections manifest? Can you cut the numbers a few different ways to show how this is possible? More importantly, what specific actions will drive this growth? When? By whom? How has that changed?" While some companies are very sophisticated in their planning processes, most small and mid-sized organizations fall short and reason something along the lines of, "Just taking Joe's word for it because he's been with us for a while and likes the same beer I do." Great leaders are not satisfied with numbers on a spreadsheet. They want to know the reasons behind the numbers.

There's a common misconception that if you write something down, it will magically happen. I've seen this more with MBAs than with any other group, thus the occasional "discrimination" when merited. There's importance in documenting goals and toggling spreadsheet data but it needs a solid foundation of logical, actionable steps. You can't increase sales by changing a number in a cell. It involves real effort. So, my advice is simple. Know that, as a Leader of Giants, action is required to get results.

Many people will overcompensate in thought for what they lack in action, so your role is to get them off the bench and on the court.

Oftentimes, belief systems are based on self-justifying low performance. When this becomes collective group thought, this leads to bad cultures that motivate employees to convince leaders they are overworked and underpaid. It can even happen in small pockets in the midst of a good culture. This is why you not only want reasons to believe in future projections; it's also why you want them to explain current results. Most often, in great companies, the employees who complain about workload are those who clash with the culture. They are usually hiding bad behaviors or "stealing" by not working earnestly according to the spirit of their agreement. The post-COVID remote-work environment has exacerbated these examples. Confidential surveys have revealed that massive numbers of employees spend very little time actually working. To hide this fact, many employees use tools to leave a perceived "footprint" of an honest workload. An early-morning email, an intentionally delayed text, and a few logins here and there can provide camouflage for a day spent at the beach.

While it would be an unfair condemnation of some companies and employees, by and large, if you had a crystal ball that allowed you to see the number of hours people actually work, it's much lower than the biggest complainers claim. When they complain about being overworked and underpaid, it's often an offensive attempt to get you not to look under the carpet. In fact, under intense scrutiny, they usually can't justify their minimal results, or the time actually put in. It is wise to take an objective look at results versus the claims of those who make the loudest complaints. Doing so will shine light on your current productivity, therefore illuminating your future path. Without a good look at what's happening, even a well-written Reasons Document will not tell the full story. Your baseline understanding of your organizational health will be the bedrock for understanding the intent of projected goals and the actions required to manifest them.

DAILY HABIT 3: BREAK YOUR MORNING DOWN TO THREE DAILY TASKS

In addition to asking for a Reasons Document, there are more things you can and should do to inspire people into action and out of vice. One way to infuse virtue and productivity into the daily operations of your organization is to help people define the three things that they must do every day to succeed. While these top three things may differ depending on position or responsibilities, they are the main drivers that create results. This is something that everybody, from the CEO down to entry-level workers, must do. In my experience, the first two should be the same for everyone.

- **First Task: Get Your Head Right**
  No matter what your role, if you're not mentally in it, you can't excel. Clear out the irrelevant and get focused. Distractions of all types hurt performance. Good news, bad news, or just plain noise can all have the same distracting effect. Your joys and problems will all be ready for you when you're done with work, so put them aside and get focused.

- **Second Task: Guard the Culture**

  Live the culture out. Be a part of what makes it a great place to work. Be the person who makes people want to work there, buy there, and post positive reviews.

- **Third Task: Do the Thing That Moves the Needle Most Before Anything Else**

  For salespeople, the thing that moves the needle is to get in front of a certain number of clients each day or week. Know what that number is and get it done. The sales will follow after the appointments are set, so get that done first. You can fix a closing percentage or average order size but only if you're in front of customers, so make it that simple.

  For CEOs, the main driver is talking to your key influencers. Who on your team do you need to check in with to make sure they have their head on straight, the culture is healthy, and key drivers are in action? If you know your leaders are highly effective and that you have provided them with the authority and resources to get their job done, then you know your primary task is set for the day. So, don't waste time on emails and data until after you know your key leaders have everything in order. These are just two examples, so determine what your key task is, and do it every day.

Realistically, these three things are not done one after another. Rather, they are done simultaneously. They are not just something to check off a list. They are what anchors the team in action. Each team member knowing what moves the needle in their role is essential. One of the top concerns for employees everywhere is, "How am I doing? What does the company think of my performance?" To create a culture that encourages motivation and problem-solving, a self-assessment mechanism needs to be in place. Some organizations have obtrusive governing systems that "keep an eye" on team members at all times, ensuring they get the job done. There are rare roles and circumstances where this may be required but it is not typically a good idea. It is best to be able to say to a team member, "Jackie, if—daily—you get your head right, guard the culture, and accomplish X, you can know what everyone thinks of your work. It will be excellent." It can be a challenge to make that statement succinct, yet the closer you come to keeping it short and simple, the better off you are. So, begin there and only add layers of complication if they are essential.

DAILY HABIT 4: KEEP PRIMARY RESPONSIBILITIES PRIMARY OR YOU WILL UNCONSCIOUSLY COMPLICATE SECONDARY RESPONSIBILITIES

You can't rely on all employees being highly virtuous people. They may not all be working toward good things for good reasons, but they can still be motivated to behave well. This is because, even though they may not love their coworkers, they probably love their Mercedes, and for that reason, they behave. This is challenging because low-virtue people can hide themselves in a crowd. They can appear to do good things for the right reasons but, at some point, they reveal themselves. Often, once a person has a certain amount of wealth or power, you start to see where they have a deficit in character. Before that, self-preservation can motivate good behaviors. The point of all this is that we often have layers of incentive that can mask our true character. We use one task as an excuse for not doing another one. Or we pay attention to certain topics, not because they are important, but because they distract us from the topics we don't like, even if those are the ones that are extremely important.

This is especially true when it comes to our primary responsibilities and our secondary responsibilities. In order to adhere to your third daily habit (break the day down to three daily tasks), you need to stay on task. That is, you need to do the third daily task before you move to lesser tasks.

If a salesperson has the primary responsibility to get five appointments every day, then their other tasks are secondary. Those would likely be some administrative things like organizing spreadsheets or cleaning out old documents. Unproductive employees, and bad leaders alike, will make secondary responsibilities more important than their primary tasks. It sounds like this:

"Hey, Bob, why didn't you get any cold calls done this week?"

"Oh, yeah. Well, I just wanted to get my expense report done."

Now, that may seem exaggerative, but if you've been in the game, you know that "expense report" is symbolic for hundreds of other equally poor excuses. Usually, it is an excuse like "doing expense reports" because they are important, and you can't argue because they need to be done. Most excuse-makers are crafty, so they use excuses that sound responsible at first blush but are easily distinguishable from legitimate reasons. The crazy thing about human nature is that Bob probably spent an enormous amount of time on his expense report, but not because it is that difficult. Rather, he made it complex in order to justify not getting his primary duties done. We all have the tendency to do this because we are human.

On the day that you do your secondary responsibilities first, you will likely never get to your primary ones. Conversely, if you do your primary responsibilities first, you will almost always have time for your secondary ones.

GIANT TAKEAWAYS

Imagine a parent saying they couldn't get around to feeding their kids because they were too busy folding laundry, working out, visiting the neighbor, or paying bills. It's an unjustified excuse full of self-justification. You must always make time for primary responsibilities, plain and simple. As a Giant, you must help your team know and act on their primary duties first. Clearly, this entire chapter rests on the shoulders of all previous ones. At the core of each of these daily habits are the Cardinal Virtues in practice, so if this is a challenge, go back and review what you've read there. Due to their power and universally applicable wisdom, you'll find something new each time you dig in.

For now, here are the Four Daily Habits for you to begin implementing right now:

- **Daily Habit 1: Bring Your Thoughts to Life with Action**
  Businesses are founded on action, not on thought alone. If you simply just take action, you'll see results. They may not always be positive results, but they will provide insight and the experience gained by execution will be valuable.

- **Daily Habit 2: Find Concrete Reasons to Believe**
  This habit applies to believing in people, looking beyond qualifications and at their character. You and your employees also must find concrete reasons to believe in projections, ideas, and plans. The best way to ensure effective actions are taken is to use a Reasons Document. In essence, this is a document that satisfies the question: *Why should I, we, you, or anyone believe your goals/plans are going to become reality?*

- **Daily Habit 3: Break Your Morning Down to Three Daily Tasks**
  Since the number one concerns of employees everywhere is, "How am I doing? What does the company think of my performance?" breaking things down into these three tasks creates a culture that encourages motivation and problem-solving.

1. **First Task:** Get your head right.
2. **Second Task:** Guard the culture.
3. **Third Task:** Do the thing that moves the needle most before anything else.

- **Daily Habit 4: Keep Primary Responsibilities Primary or You Will Unconsciously Complicate Secondary Responsibilities**
Most excuse-makers are crafty, so they use excuses that sound responsible at first blush but are easily distinguishable from legitimate reasons. We all have the tendency to do this because we are human, but a Giant knows better and knows how to spot this lack of virtue.

10

Love Your People to Success

In a meeting during the early years of forming a new business, my partners, key leaders, and I were discussing managing growth and how to permeate our culture and standards into a rapidly increasing head count. Several sharp execs proposed effective ways to accomplish this task. However, at a certain point, the conversation moved almost exclusively in the direction of technology and programs. The ideas they suggested held value and would be used, but not going deeper than implementing programs or technology ran the risk of sending the message that our culture and standards would be communicated in an automated way. Having had this experience prior, I knew we needed more. It was paramount to communicate the culture the way we intended it to be lived out. I said, "It's this simple: we've got to love our people to success." Sensing that the wording sounded a bit warm and fuzzy, I went to say, with a wink, "If anyone here thinks that's a soft approach, I want you to know that I love my kids so much that I am willing to make them cry."

The Thomistic definition of love is to "will the good of the other." This is the most powerful definition of love I know. Great parents, for the good of their children, discipline them for bad behaviors. Doing so, as all parents know, can lead to tears. Weak parents fear the conflict that comes from correcting children, so they do everything to make their children happy in the moment without considering the long-term effects. Ironically, this makes both parent and child very unhappy and difficult to be around. The analogy breaks down only in the sense that team members are not children and, as such, they deserve a certain type of respect. However, the principle still holds true, and because our human nature doesn't change at any age, I will use the parenting analogy again simply because it is easy to understand.

Loving your people to success is what creates and sustains a great culture. It's what should guide and direct your decision-making on every level. Ultimately, it's a major component to unlocking your ability to develop anyone into a Giant. Philosophers and theologians would be able to articulate a fuller description of love, but for the practical purpose of understanding love at the leadership level, there are four ways to show that you love someone. In other words, these are the ways you can effectively love your people to success in the workplace:

1. Sacrifice
2. Security
3. Independence
4. Empowerment

SACRIFICE

If you think you're *in* love, how do you know? If you think you *are* loved, how do you know? The answer is simpler than it may seem. If sacrifice is present, it's very likely that it is true love. Imagine a man claiming to love his wife but who is never willing to sacrifice. She asks him, "Do you love me?" and he says, "Of course I do." To which she replies, "How come you never say 'I love you'? How come you never help around the house and just sit around and watch TV? How come, when I am mentally or emotionally in pain, you don't ask how I feel or comfort me? How come you don't help with the kids or provide for our financial needs?" If these things are true, and yet he claims to love her, he's lying.

Sacrificial love has rich meaning, texture, and depth, uniting us in good, true, and beautiful ways to those we know. Inordinate love of self, ego, and self-centeredness are also strong motivating forces used by some people in relationships, but because they're shallow they never win in the long run. To will the good of another is the ultimate act of love, because it involves sacrifice and investment in the lives of others. The first sacrifice to make to ensure a great relationship is becoming your best self, because you can't give what you don't have. The second is to provide an environment for your team to do the same.

Furthermore, love is like talent; it needs a stage, or an opportunity to live it out. You can't claim to be a great musician having never picked up an instrument. If you are a great musician but you never play, then your lack of commitment makes your talent irrelevant. Love always has a target. The stage in the workplace is where you meet; the target is your colleagues. Make sacrifices by not living for the fulfillment of your own ego but understand that what people want most from you is for you to take them where they need and want to go.

SECURITY

When a child feels safe with their parents, at some point, they recognize that correction and discipline are an act of love. At first, a young person may want their parents to allow deviant or promiscuous behaviors, but as they mature, a sense of disappointment arises. This usually happens when the pain caused from harmful behaviors sets in. Passivity on the part of the parent is not love; it's weakness. Clearly, from a sacrificial perspective, being willing to endure the anger, frustration, and even tears of a teenager is an act of love. But there's more to it. The corrections, when done out of love, provide a sense of safety and security, and they convey, "I value you and I will protect you."

While these parental examples continue to fall short, simply due to the fact that professional relationships are adult to adult versus adult to child, the similarities are important. When your team knows that you want what is best for them—aka you will their good—they feel secure when you correct them.

Some days, being a leader can seem harsh, but even those tough moments are compassionate when they are done correctly. If someone did something that merits firing and they're feeling insecure, don't placate them. Letting them feel bad because they need to work through their wrongdoing can be the fuel for change. However, if someone works earnestly and makes an honest mistake, it's best to help them feel secure. Loving that person to success, you'd say something like, "You're doing good work and made an honest mistake. I'm not holding this against you. I want you to freely come into work with enthusiasm, unafraid of making reasonable mistakes in the future, and continue to succeed. Just learn from it so you can avoid this specific mistake in the future."

In cases where someone lied or manipulated someone or a situation, but the action didn't entirely merit termination, let them sit in their insecurity. You might say something like, "This is a big deal, and it can't happen again. If it does, I'll have no choice but to let you go. The ice underneath your feet is very thin. Every single day that goes by, the pond can freeze a little more, until there's thick ice underneath you. But for a little while, I don't mind you being a bit uneasy because that's what this calls for." As a Leader of Giants, you need to uphold top behavior. Those tough conversations are what it looks like to love your people to success because they combine standards, Justice, and mercy.

INDEPENDENCE

When my children were young, I remember being told by an elderly man who had already passed the test of raising great kids, "Dave, you are not raising children. You are raising future adults, so do all things with the end in mind to shape them for that role." The goal of a parent should be to lead children to become independent, moral, and responsible adults who can and will make the right choices in life that positively contribute to others. Leading a team is not much different, but in business, you're raising up future Giants. As people evolve in your organization, they'll increase in power, influence, and function.

A Leader of Giants wants and needs people to operate with independence. This should not be confused with being lone wolves or operating on islands and in silos. It means you can think for yourself because you know how to think. That means asking for advice or seeking more knowledge if you fall short. It's being able to rely on others when needed but not depending on them for everything. Independent employees who act and behave in accordance with the betterment of others in mind will yield a winning culture with extraordinary results.

EMPOWERMENT

Leadership requires distributing power. Great leaders are eager to empower their teams and do so as quickly as possible. You empower your team with several things. The first is authority. Giving someone authority reduces your workload and increases your influence. When someone speaks with your authority, it's like being in more than one place at a time, which is key to leveraging and expanding influence. The second way to empower them is with tools and resources that help them implement the decisions they make. Among the most powerful resources to give someone is the power to delegate. When someone under your authority delegates to someone under his or her authority, you have now exponentially increased your influence. Clearly, you must determine that the person you empower is trustworthy, which is something you won't fully know until he or she is exercising that authority, but waiting too long or never taking the risk guarantees failure.

LOVE NEVER FAILS

When I say, "Love your people to success," it's said with passion and purpose. I've never said this casually or offhandedly. In business, the word *love* is understandably not used often. Workplace relationships require clear boundaries, and the "love" shared is about respect and camaraderie, shown through mentorship, support, and recognition of achievements. However, both in professional and personal contexts, love is confronting, and it can lead to real pain if misused or misunderstood.

The ancient Greeks identified seven distinct types of love: *philia* (friendship), *storge* (family), *eros* (romance), *ludus* (playful), *pragma* (long-standing love), *agape* (selfless love), and *philautia* (self-love). So, when I say to "love your people to success," the kind of love I'm speaking of is a combination of *agape, philia, pragma,* and *storge*. In a way, our coworkers become a second family (*storge*), and loyalty (*pragma*) is priceless in building a successful business. While it's essential to have friends outside of work, the friendship (*philia*) shared in a healthy workplace culture can be greatly uplifting. A culture based on selfless actions (*agape*) is what will determine the depth and quality of love shared in your organization. And it all starts with you. What kind of leader are you going to be? Will you hold people accountable? Will you ask for help when you need it? Are you going to fire the passive-aggressive manager or keep turning a blind eye?

By loving your people to success, you will be looking out for ways to instill virtue, goodness, truth, beauty, and unity in those you lead, which is hard to do most of the time. But doing so is crucial, especially during hard times, such as when taking disciplinary action, having confronting conversations, closing divisions or departments, or firing someone. When you love your people to success, even the hardest of times are bearable.

Making sacrifices allows you to evolve and grow alongside someone more rapidly and effectively. That doesn't mean you should lose yourself by making unreasonable sacrifices. Joy is usually present at some level when sacrifice is done out of love. That's a good test: Sacrifice + Joy = Genuine Love. Someone who seems to be highly sacrificial but has no joy and puts their sacrifice on display, expecting something in return, is problematic. That's usually a sign that they're insincere, and that sacrifice typically stops when they don't get what they want. The more you will the good of others, the more you begin to access your full potential as a leader.

SERVANT LEADERSHIP

I've mentioned this many times throughout the book, but I'll say it again: *a great leader takes you where you need and want to go.* That's it. When you get on a plane, you want a great pilot. Upon meeting them, they may be a suave communicator and make you feel 100% safe. So, you take your seat, thinking of what an extraordinary pilot you have. You boarded in Chicago and are headed to Denver, but when you land, you've arrived in Charlotte! They're not a great pilot after all, simply because they didn't take you to where you needed to go.

> *Weak people are willing to be led by*
> *other weak people, but Giants only*
> *want to be led by other Giants.*

When a good leader takes people where they need to go, this will inevitably include guiding them through necessary suffering. Most people would like to appear as if they're loving people to their success, so they flatter, bluff, or make false "sacrifices." Flattery, placating, making things easy for people to satisfy them, doing a job for them, or reducing all of their problems is not a part of good leadership. Leadership is equipping people with the proper tools, resources, and authority to solve problems on their own. It's not fishing for them; it's teaching them how to fish.

Loving your people to success and being a servant leader does not mean that if you're a coach, you have to run laps with the team. A failure to lead would be more like handing them all an ice cream and telling them to take a break. A servant leader expects the best from his team because that's what is best for them. It's knowing what they want but more importantly what they need, and leading them to it, even (and especially) if it means taking them through suffering to get there. You'll know you're doing it well if, even amid the growing pains, an ultimate sense of joy is present, and safety is felt by all involved.

A HYPOCRITE VS. A WEAK PERSON

From the beginning of time, one of the greatest human pastimes is pointing out hypocrites. Most of the time, the accusation is false and is done as a deflection. "Don't look at me. Look at them. Look at how bad they are," the accuser says. Other times, perceived hypocrisy is more of an observation of weakness than anything else, and there is a difference. The reason I tell you this is because I have observed many aspiring Giants make poor decisions under the fear of being called a hypocrite. If you do, you might act less powerful than you should, and you definitely won't be focused on loving your people to success.

So, let's break this down. A cardiologist who smokes cigarettes and says, "I can't tell my patients not to smoke because I smoke," fails to do his job. He has a moral obligation to tell them that they shouldn't smoke. He is not a hypocrite; he's a weak person. There's no doubt that weak people do lose influence, but being weak doesn't equate to being a hypocrite. A weak person may not be strong enough to take his own advice, but he believes he should. Whereas a hypocrite is a person who says that you should do things they don't even believe in. Hypocrites are insincere, like the corrupt politician or "philanthropist" who says you shouldn't drive a sports car or use a gas stove, and yet they fly to each climate speech on a private jet after vacationing on their mega-yacht.

It's a waste of time to point out hypocrisy because hypocrites won't listen. Fundamentally, a hypocrite is a propagandist, and on some level, they know that what they're saying is nonsense. The guy who takes his private jet to climate change speeches is going to keep doing it no matter what you say. (Note: I have a private jet, and I love it! But I don't call a press conference telling people to ride bikes to work while I'm boarding my plane.) When confronted, they're just going to try to hide the lie better, but they don't care. They will still buy a bigger jet, drive SUVs, and burn gas stoves in all 12 of their homes while expecting you to give up meat because of the methane emissions made by cattle. The hypocritical propagandist presumes you're stupid in the first place and that they're smarter. Because of this, they have the fatal flaw of pride, which is the very thing that gets them to brazenly do unbelievably arrogant and stupid things. Thankfully, most of us are weak people, like the cigarette-addicted doctor, and are not hypocrites.

A weak person has a moral obligation to tell people to do things that they are too weak to do themselves. You will hear parents say, "Who am I to tell my kids not to smoke, drink, or sleep around?" The answer to that question is . . . YOU'RE THEIR PARENT! You can't make decisions about the well-being of your children based on the mistakes of your past. If you now know, in your maturity, that those things harmed you, then you must direct your kids. As a leader, you must see the best in those you lead, asking, "How great can they be?" If that question is asked in light of how great you were in the past, you will never lead anyone past your own historical performance. Even worse, that approach can often bring a potentially high-performing person to new lows.

Take another situation I have seen often, which is the salesperson who was promoted to sales manager because he was charismatic and gregarious but not necessarily a high performer. He wasn't that driven as a salesperson so he feels like he can't tell his people to get a lot of appointments, which he never did. So, he thinks, *Who am I to enforce the very standards that I didn't adhere to?* He drags his team down due to his own previous low standards. The fact is, he is the sales manager, and he has an obligation to tell his team to maximize their schedules regardless of his history. He clearly can't lie by claiming he performed beyond his track record, but frankly, his track record isn't that relevant.

Don't take yourself out of the game because you're afraid of being called a hypocrite. You are weak. We all are. See the best in others and work with them to attain their own greatness according to who they are, not according to your history.

GIANT TAKEAWAYS

Loving your people to success is what will create and sustain a great culture. It's what should guide and direct your decision-making on every level. Ultimately, it's the key that unlocks your ability to develop anyone into a Giant. Here are four ways to know that you revere someone, or in this instance, that you are effectively loving your people to success in the workplace:

1. **Sacrifice:** To will the good of the other is the ultimate act of love, because it involves sacrifice and investment in the lives of others. Sacrifice is part of what makes an ordinary leader a Giant. The first sacrifice is to suffer the discipline of becoming your best self. The second is to provide an environment for others to do the same.

2. **Security:** When your team knows that you want what is best for them, they'll feel secure when you correct them. As a Leader of Giants, you need to uphold top behavior by having tough conversations and shutting down culture-eroding behaviors.

3. **Independence:** A Giant wants and needs people to operate with independence. This should not be confused with being a lone wolf or operating on an island. It means thinking for yourself because you know how to think, including asking for advice or seeking more knowledge if you fall short.

4. **Empowerment:** Empower your team with authority along with tools and resources so they can implement the decisions they make. When they are doing so on your behalf, you must determine that the person you empower is trustworthy, which is something you won't fully know until he or she is exercising that authority. But waiting too long or never taking the risk guarantees failure.

The presence or absence of joy, from both participants, is how you can know the depth and quality of love, or in a workplace setting, camaraderie, respect, loyalty, truthfulness, and the like. Remember, in both your professional and personal life: Sacrifice + Joy = Genuine Love.

Last but not least, give attention to the fact that, sometimes, you are weak. We all are. Overcome this by seeing the best in others, working with them to attain their own greatness according to who they are, not according to your history.

Love is the foundation of building a great culture, a topic we will cover in depth throughout the next four chapters.

11

Market Your Culture Daily

*To be prepared for war is one of the most effective means
of preserving peace.*

—George Washington

A common organizational tool used to establish culture has been the mission statement. Peter Drucker popularized the idea in the mid '70s, and by the '90s, it became a standard. Over the years, we've also seen other trends like core values, company visions, and KRAs go in and out of vogue. In the late '80s and '90s, the intensity with which mission statements were constructed was unforgettable. Large organizations had full-page, detailed missions, with specific yet tenuous wording . . . all for nothing. Executives who had massive salaries would be taken on a mission statement formation retreat, wasting excessive amounts of money, only to leave not knowing the point of the meeting. These word-salad mission statements were posted on walls in the break room, serving more as a banner of dysfunction than something that meant anything to anyone.

One time, I was invited to speak for a Fortune 10 business that I'll keep unnamed. The leader of a large division asked me via his deputies to talk to the employees about productivity and teamwork. They had recently merged with another industry leader, and blending the teams was not going well. I only agreed to do so if I could work with the top brass, where the problems began in the first place. The leaders, by way of the deputies, agreed.

When I began my presentation for the division of several hundred employees, I said, "I'd like all of us to stand up and say the mission statement together as if we were reciting the Pledge of Allegiance." Panic set in as none of them, literally not one person, knew the mission statement. I'd quickly let everyone know they didn't really have to, and the executives were especially grateful that I let them off the hook. Their mission statement was esoteric, obscure, impossible to memorize, and uninspiring. No one could recite the statement because no one felt connected to it. At this particular organization, like many others, the leadership knew the importance of culture, but due to so many changes, had no idea how to enact, maintain, or develop it.

The purpose of a mission statement should be to get a group of diverse people on the same page and moving in the same direction. In one sense, a great culture is ironically meant to diminish the "diversity" of an organization. If everyone is so different that they don't have any similar values, the mission can't be fulfilled. You can't go to war if your army roots for your enemy or runs in their own direction. So, while it is crucial to not discriminate, a major goal of leadership is alignment. This is accomplished much better if our universal human nature is considered when forming a mission and making other decisions. Among other things, we all like to feel significant, recognized, needed, appreciated, rewarded, respected, and challenged. Obviously, we also all have a desire for unity, goodness, truth, and beauty. So, tying a mission into something that fulfills those desires allows a diverse team to gel, while using differences to enhance instead of separate.

If diversity is put ahead of unity,
the result is merely division.

As I said in the previous chapter, most people identify with a leader who is not a hypocrite, leads by example, is a servant leader, and many other good things. But really, as I mentioned earlier, what makes a leader great is they take people where they want and need to go. A mission statement is an aid for leadership, providing people with direction toward where they want and need to go.

SURE, HAVE A MISSION STATEMENT, BUT FOCUS MORE ON THIS . . .

What's far more useful than a mission statement is a cultural statement. Mission statements are oftentimes exaggerative, like "Our mission is to be the most respected, widely admired, and number one paper clip maker in the entire world." For the most part, that only gets the owner fired up because nobody else cares that much about paper clips. What people do care about is being on a winning team and being at the top of their field. That's something that creates an empowered culture. Sometimes it's enough to be passionate about the product, and that can drive and inspire the culture. But most always, a passion for building, organizing, and winning is what gets everyone truly inspired.

If you're a pro football team, your mission is to win the Super Bowl. It's such a powerful mission that it starts with the owner and pulls in fans from far and wide. That's a mission so large and clearly defined that people get behind it. Yet, even with such a huge mission, it's still the role of the owner, general manager, and coach to instill a winning culture. There are examples of one-off championship runs by professional sports teams; however, the dynasty teams are proven to be a result of a strong organizational culture.

Most people don't get a job because they're passionate about the product. If you asked someone, "Tell me, what do you think of paper clips?" you won't hear, "Oh, they've been my passion since I was a child! Some kids would be playing outside, wanting to be pro athletes, but not me. I wanted to sell *paper clips*!" That's not to say you won't meet people who are completely invested in their job and doing fantastic work at Paper Clips Inc. Their commitment comes from the opportunity to win via the paper clips. The goal of winning together is what creates an extraordinary culture, and that starts at the top regardless of the product or service.

As I alluded to earlier, many leaders fail to see that there are universal preferences and aspirations, in part based on human nature. A terrific 2007 article in the *Harvard Business Review* titled "What It Means to Work Here," by Tamara J. Erickson and Lynda Gratton, is a timeless illustration that points to the importance of promoting cultural statements internally.[1] They note that in addition to things like competitive compensation, people "choose jobs—and, more important, become engaged with their work—on the basis of how well their preferences and aspirations mesh with those of the organization." Beyond basic provision, benefits, and stability, people want two things to derive purpose from their work, whether they know it or not.

These are:

1. To be on the side of winning, aka to be an industry leader.
2. To be convinced that by working with you, they're personally going to be transformed for the better.

As you've heard me repeat, a good bumper sticker saying I have provided my senior leadership teams amid establishing winning cultures based on human nature is, "It's not what you do for work that matters as much as who you become while you're doing it." Understanding human nature, natural law, virtue, and vice are the most effective ways to develop leadership intuition and genuine influence. So then, what are some of these universal preferences and aspirations?

1. The need to feel respected and appreciated (i.e., ample recognition).
2. The need to be valued for what you meritoriously bring to the table, such as intellect, skill, experience, and insight (i.e., not race, creed, sex, or who you sleep with, which, unless you're sexist or racist, say nothing about your skill or preparedness).
3. The need to be given autonomy in proportion to experience and results (i.e., merit).
4. The need to be supported and trained in proportion to any lack of knowledge, skill, and talent.
5. The opportunity to advance but not the pressure to do so if that is not prioritized.
6. The need to feel reasonably protected and secure. The feeling that "We have your back" when making decisions (assuming good intent and Prudence were reasonably applied).
7. The need to be compensated justly.

In regard to human nature, Aristotle taught that because humans have reason and language in our soul, we are meant to achieve our best. For the most part, the responsibility of an organization is to provide an environment for this to be possible. The contemporary and very popular saying "Be the best version of yourself" reflects the universal appeal of this idea and fortifies what Aristotle taught more than 2,300 years ago. Making sure these seven universal aspirations and preferences are woven into your organizational culture is paramount.

THE BONES OF A CULTURAL STATEMENT

The cultural statement applies to every person in the company. It defines the essence of your business. Put metaphorically, it's the vibe of the party. Writing a cultural statement need not be complex.

It is wise to emulate other companies that have written and enacted great cultural statements. For a couple of my first companies, I took parts of Southwest Airlines' statement because it was one of the most culturally admired organizations in the world. Cultures can ebb and flow, but back then, they had a 40-year track record of leading the stock market. Much of that was due to their culture. They had exceptionally strong leadership, a simple mission, and a brilliant cultural statement.

So, what are the core components of a cultural statement? In my opinion, it must first say something about the Fortitude and will you wish to permeate the organization. This could be written as, "We are willing to own our failures in order to have the right to own our successes." In addition to that, it needs to speak to how people interact with each other. "We bring a fun-loving spirit to work every day," or "We work with a compassionate heart," or "We always assume the best in each other" are all ways to enact professional dialogue. Then, define the virtues that guide the workplace. It could be that it's important that everyone has fun together, or that the company is centered on humility, truth, or Fortitude. Here is an example of an effective cultural statement. (Note: The bold portions are all that's needed for the actual statement. The bullet points are the way you would talk about it and promote it by example.)

We strive to:

1. **Be humble.**
   - We offer unbiased, precise truth about ourselves and situations, good or bad.

2. **Have a compassionate heart.**
   - Without false romanticism, we assume the best in others and see/dwell on the good.
3. **Have a strong professional will.**
   - We persist when things are difficult and own our mistakes in order to have a right to take credit for our wins.
4. **Bring a fun-loving spirit to work.**
   - If you're going to be here, you might as well make it fun, appropriate to the setting. Own the vibe you bring to the table versus criticizing others.

The most important part of a mission statement or cultural statement is setting the expectations of behaviors. Strategies, markets, competition, personnel, budgets, and many other things will change, but the way in which the people on the team behave will determine the success of the organization. All things being equal, the team who collectively demonstrates the greatest virtue will win. So, make virtue a core part of what you communicate, and communicate it often, with great enthusiasm.

Simply maintaining a great culture isn't enough because cultures erode 1% a day if you don't continuously develop them.

DIG DEEP AND DEFEND YOUR CULTURE

It is important to set the stage for your culture and do so immediately, consistently, and confidently. This is why I chose George Washington's words to begin this chapter: "To be prepared for war is one of the most effective means of preserving peace." When you prepare candidates for what it truly means to work in your organization, you begin setting the stage for peace, order, and prosperity. Although we all have an innate and universal desire to become our best self, this desire can be suppressed or put in a coma the same way that a conscience can become malformed. Candidates who are accustomed to vices such as laziness, lying, gossip, and victimhood will be repelled by a good culture because it would require them to make too many difficult changes. On the other hand, those who are actively interested in becoming their best self will be very attracted to a healthy culture. Those in the middle will likely find it mildly appealing. This is good news for you because you eliminate the bad candidates, attract the great ones, and have the power to influence and mold those in the middle.

No matter how great your culture is, it will always be challenged. Great leaders protect their organizations from predatory manipulators. Every organization will have stronger and weaker members. Eventually there will be enemies on the inside. Most would not call themselves enemies and some may not even know they are being destructive, but they will erode the culture due to their vice. Great leaders build a culture that protects itself because they know they won't always be present to do so.

The greatest way to protect yourself, and succeed, is to be formidable—being prepared for war but always choosing peace. This is also one of the reasons that studies show women are naturally attracted to and like men who are powerful. Power can be misused, but for Giants, who are virtuous, they wield it in such a way that everyone knows that if a line is crossed, they are willing and capable of fighting . . . and winning. It must never be forgotten that strength and formidability require the restraint and moral compass that is found in the practice of the Cardinal Virtues.

There's a saying that "absolute power corrupts absolutely." It's a false statement. Absolute power can corrupt, and does quite often, but it doesn't do it absolutely. There's no greater form of leadership than a person who has absolute power *and* has your best interest and their interests fully aligned. In that environment, you're protected, enabled, and empowered by that person.

In business, fending off a threat is not done physically. It's done intellectually, and it's done through having a strong professional will—essentially, it's done through grit. When your organization is strong, and has a powerful cultural statement and an established culture, it's like an immune system that fights off disease. Not only can people within the organization attempt to destroy the culture, but people on the outside can try to by threatening lawsuits or cowardly tainting your reputation online. The stronger you are, the less willing they will be to threaten your organization.

PULLING IT ALL TOGETHER

When it comes to mission statements, most executives go a little over the top. They don't say this directly, but they often sound like, "We are an excellent company, with excellent standards, and we all act excellent all the time." In stark contrast, a healthy cultural statement conveys the message that *"We're a bunch of imperfect people working toward perfection,"* without saying so directly. A problem that most people have experienced is hearing big talk about culture in a job interview only to find out once they begin working there that it was a facade. So, being sincere about your culture is crucial. This is why I caution you against using phrases like "we all are humble" and advise instead saying "we strive for humility." Demonstrating the room for error and giving grace for bad days is important to prevent hypocrisy and finger-pointing, and to relieve the pressure to be perfect.

You'll also notice that a clear and concise cultural statement says nothing about a product, data, or profit. Instead, its function is to remind everyone why and how they should be working there. However, it runs the risk of being a wall decoration if it's not constantly enforced. A cultural statement requires that people internalize what it says as well as constantly guard the culture, reminding others to do the same. Once your new hires begin their role, it is important to reiterate the cultural statement and do so by highlighting good examples, rewarding actions aligned with the culture. This acts as an opportunity to recognize current employees, therefore satisfying some of their universal preferences and inspiring others to emulate the behavior. Humans have a mimetic desire to have what others have, which is why two toddlers will often be in a room ignoring a toy until one of them picks it up. Then, simply because one of them made it important, the other now finds it desirable. Recognition is the same for us as adults and you can ignite this in positive ways for others. A problem can arise when a new hire emulates good behaviors but is not thanked or recognized for it. They may feel disenchanted, so be sure to actively reinforce good behaviors. Certainly, all of this can be overdone, leading to an insatiable appetite for recognition, so do all things within reason.

I recommend reminding your team of the cultural statement, in one way or another, during every weekly call or meeting. Even small daily anecdotes are valuable. The point is this: it is nearly impossible to talk about culture too often. Marketing your culture requires promoting it daily. You can't just give one "cultural" talk at a meeting and then go on your way. Marketing your culture daily may even mean doing lesser but important things like putting the cultural statement on coffee mugs or encoding it into your logos. Any way to influence others to adopt the culture will only empower and uplift your organization.

Keep in mind that your culture's growth will be accelerated by the way you live it out. Being a humble, strong-willed, compassionate, and fun-loving leader will say more than a wall poster or mug. The trust your team has in you and the organization because you exhibit what you promote will come in handy because right when everything seems to be going perfectly, problems will arise that you've never faced. I'll show you next how a healthy culture actually prevents problems, allowing you to focus your time and energy on what truly matters, such as self-mastery, innovation, or shoring up deficiencies, instead of managing a never-ending stream of self-inflicted problems.

GIANT TAKEAWAYS

- The purpose of a mission statement should be to get a group of diverse people on the same page and moving in the same direction. They are valuable only if they are concise and motivating. A far better tool is a cultural statement.
- Beyond basic provision, benefits, and stability, people want two things to derive purpose from their work, whether they know it or not: (1) to be on the side of winning—aka to be an industry leader—and (2) to be convinced that by working with you, they're personally going to be transformed for the better.
- The seven universal preferences and aspirations are how to understand human nature, natural law, virtue, and vice, and are the most effective ways to develop leadership intuition and genuine influence.
- All things being equal, the team who collectively demonstrates the greatest virtue will win. So, make virtue a core part of what you communicate, and communicate it often, with great enthusiasm!
- The greatest way to protect yourself, and succeed, is to be formidable—being prepared for war but always choosing peace. When your organization is strong, and has a powerful cultural statement and an established culture, it's like an immune system that fights off disease.
- Remind your team of the cultural statement, in one way or another, during every weekly call or meeting. It is nearly impossible to talk about culture too often.

In addition to writing a new cultural statement, after reading this chapter, list below five things you need to do to give your culture the foundation it needs:

1. _____

2. _____

3. _____

4. _____

5. _____

A Healthy Culture Prevents Problems

Intellectuals solve problems, geniuses prevent them.

—Albert Einstein

To avoid bad practices eroding your culture or reputation, remember: "It's not what you do for work that matters as much as who you become while you're doing it." Another way to say this is, "It's not what you do, it's how you go about it that matters." There are limitless ways to be immoral, even nefarious, in business. Therefore, having ways to not only avoid bad behaviors but to create good behaviors is essential. A great culture is the best way to make that happen. A winning culture comprised of Giants will keep things running smoothly, allowing you to focus on leading rather than constantly managing problems.

Problems are inevitable, but when left unchecked they can grow, leading to massive chaos. If a company has core problematic issues, it is likely that vice permeates the culture, leading to an unproductive workplace and poor decision-making. Cultural problems are like threads that can be pulled on, risking it all coming unraveled. On the other hand, when a problem manifests in a virtue-based organization, like a well-made rug, a single thread does not threaten the whole's integrity. A strong culture is like having safety knots tied and interwoven throughout so when a thread comes loose—i.e., when a person or situation becomes problematic—it only unravels to the closest knot, keeping things secure and intact.

Decisive action is required to strengthen a great culture. Skilled leaders know there are times to use humor, kid gloves, and deflection to get people back on track. Other times, you must swiftly and decisively shut down negative manipulations or nefarious actions. The good news is that most problems arise out of reasonable ignorance, miscommunication, or even zeal for improvement, in which case your team should know that leaders have their backs. They should feel confident and even protected when they make earnest mistakes. Giants encourage their people to work hard and have the confidence to make decisions knowing that they are all in a different phase of maturation when it comes to the Cardinal Virtues and personal growth. If in that process a mistake is made, Giants know it's likely easily resolved and the lessons learned will make the company stronger.

When growing a winning culture, there will be opposite ends of a proverbial spectrum when it comes to people within the company. On one hand, there will be people who don't fit the culture, including the rare person who tries to wag the dog. These people are vice ridden and are generally too weak or insecure to own their mistakes, so they pass off blame to others or manipulate situations (I offer a further description of these types of people in chapter 16; they are called Egotistical Individual Players, or EIPs). People like that need swift and firm correction. On the other hand, there will be people who fit the culture but who are works in progress (also referenced in chapter 16 as Team Players, TPs; and Ambitious Team Players, ATPs). These people primarily need encouragement. The combination of encouragement for the people who fit the culture, and firm correction for those who don't, does three powerful things. First, it spits out those who don't fit the culture like antibodies discarding unwanted substances to keep a person healthy. Vice-laden people are often so hardened that, when given the choice to improve or quit, they choose the latter. Second, it converts some of them into loyal members because they are attracted to the strength and conviction of the leaders. There's nothing more attractive than strength. Vice-laden but not yet hardened people will see a strong leader and healthy culture as a lifeboat toward a happier life. So, despite testing their luck at first, they can become loyal converts. Lastly, it fortifies the resolve of those who are already loyal to continue to improve and evangelize the culture. Those who accept a great culture begin to own it for themselves, therefore promoting and guarding it. They know they are contributing to what makes their organization a great place to work and take healthy pride in their contribution.

An organization's culture should be felt in every department. To the degree that leadership fosters a great culture, each division leader will develop his or her department's own unique flavor, but that flavor will pair well with the overall culture. Furthermore, the cultures that live deep within any organization will spill out into the customer and client experience. Low quality engineering standards, a crooked finance department, slow fulfillment, and deceitful sales practices all find their way to the end user, client, or point of sale.

Because silos and turf wars can naturally develop among departments, it is important to create a culture that encourages self-correction. Tensions occur between departments when leadership inadvertently sets up incentives to compete against one another. For example, this often happens between sales and production or sales and fulfillment because both departments feel immense competing pressures. Sales leaders often feel the pressure of bonus deadlines and commission schedules, so they try to "hit their numbers." Conversely, production and fulfillment departments are often recognized and incentivized for delivering quality products and services on time. If the sales team sells an unrealistic timeline, then production and fulfillment feel set up to fail. If production and fulfillment don't deliver on time, then sales leaders often accuse them of "ruining" the sale. So, both departments "fight" due to opposing incentives. Sales wants things fast; production wants things to go slower. This sort of tension can lead to infighting and low morale. As a Leader of Giants, align incentives by helping departments see the union between each role and share in the joint effort to provide the client a positive experience. A potential solution for this is to bonus production for increased efficiency or have them participate in the sales process. Or, conversely, bonus the salespeople for on-time deliveries, thereby aligning their sales outcomes to a realistic production timeline.

THE SURPRISINGLY DISPROPORTIONATE IMPACT SALES HAS ON CULTURE

It is a good idea to understand culture through the eyes of the sales team because, ultimately, they hand off a product to clients. While the product has relative significance, how it's bought and sold is a result of the culture. Through that lens, sales leaders have huge responsibilities for recruiting the right team, prospecting (lead generation), presentation approaches and materials, closing the sale, upselling, and retaining past customers and clients. Each of the decisions made to manage these responsibilities will produce a "feeling" by the customer. That feeling is a big part of what makes a brand. The way sales and customer service teams are treated by the company will determine how they treat clients and customers. And the way customers are treated by salespeople and customer service representatives will determine how customers treat the company. Online reviews, which are often an outcome of the client–sales experience, have tremendous power to alter attitudes and morale within the ranks of any organization.

Peter Drucker famously said that "culture eats strategy for breakfast." This is true, and it can be expounded upon by saying that a great culture will always (eventually) produce great strategy. This is because a great culture puts the best minds in an atmosphere where people make great decisions (Prudence), make fair policies (Justice), overcome difficult challenges (Fortitude), and keep morale positive and uplifting (Temperance). Additionally, cultures thrive off those who are humble, hungry for greatness, and team oriented. When all those things happen within a culture, negative things won't grow and manifest. With a healthy culture, rarely do unfit people rise to high levels of authority. Bad ideas generally don't prevail, and pride is normally left at the door.

When it comes to a healthy sales culture, you must establish organizational respect for salespeople. Sadly, I see many companies get this wrong. They either neglect sales or mock those who are in it, making them adversaries, not allies. Not only does this run the risk of your salespeople leaving for your competitors, but it also risks destroying the good name of your company if the people who interface with customers are unhappy. An unhappy salesperson sends an unconscious message to prospects that something is awry. This is a bizarre commonality when considering that salespeople make it possible for everyone to be paid. Clearly, some companies have such tremendous products that sales are relatively easy. Other companies have such brilliant marketing teams that, again, sales come easy. But those examples are usually short-lived and are not the norm, so they require almost no discussion. In most businesses, salespeople and sales programs have a disproportionate role in success or failure. Since culture has the potential to travel into and out of most organizations via the sales process, ensuring sales team members are respected is a great priority.

Another common problem that can destabilize a healthy sales culture is jealousy. When executives try competing with salespeople for attention, problems arise. If someone who works in the C-suite for a record label gets jealous of the star performer, they all lose. Being a Giant, you know the order of things. You also know all departments should be valued equally but not the same way. While stress and pressure are present in any important role, salespeople, and especially commission-based salespeople, experience rejection at levels much greater than any other role. Although the stakes are high in accounting and their impact can be grave, they are not as frequently or relentlessly in your face as they are in sales. In accounting, you don't have income statements telling you "no" every 15 minutes. You get paid if the income statement has an item in the wrong line and needs an adjustment or if it is done perfectly the first time, albeit these errors can certainly threaten the longevity of the person making them.

Great salespeople should be treated with a certain respect because *everyone* in the business needs them forging ahead, bringing energy into the system. When salespeople enter the building, I recommend an attitude resembling "officer on deck" because, in some way, they're paying the bills and funding payroll. If sales go, so does your job, and so does everything else. If you don't recognize that, you're missing the point of who the salespeople are. If a sales team is berated, diminished, or hamstrung by administration or production, it might feel good for a moment, but it's a lose-lose situation to knock down the officer on deck. Cultures, regardless of industry, are primarily driven by vice or virtue; however, a healthy sales culture has a disproportionate role in permeating the rest of the company culture. If you protect the attitudes, energy, and opportunity for your sales teams, you will ease tensions that you might not know stem from a lack of sales support.

Unsurprisingly, the core of building a winning culture of Giants is found by instilling virtue. Due to human nature and our tendency to stray toward vice, the best way to prevent problems is to ask questions that utilize the Cardinal Virtues. These foundational questions, for example, will shine light on core practices that will govern everything from sales to admin:

- What should we sell? (Prudence)
- How should we sell it? What is our complete value chain? (Prudence)
- How do we pay our teams? (Justice)
- What do we charge for our product or service? (Justice)
- How do we motivate our teams? (Fortitude)
- How do we keep them motivated? (Temperance)
- How do we manage our financial department? (all four Cardinal Virtues)

While these are basic questions, there are countless other questions that, as a leader, you are likely asking yourself in the process of founding, scaling, or leading your company. To find answers to these and all other questions, you could pay a consultant thousands of dollars, implement strategies, and enforce new programs . . . or embrace that your best answers come via good habits learned by exercising virtue.

GIANT TAKEAWAYS

A great culture is the best way to not only avoid bad behaviors but to create good behaviors. A winning culture comprised of Giants will keep things running smoothly, allowing you to focus on leading rather than constantly managing problems. Most problems arise out of reasonable ignorance, miscommunication, or even zeal for improvement, in which case your team should know that leaders have their backs. The combination of encouragement for the people who fit the culture, and firm correction for those who don't, does three powerful things:

1. It spits out those who don't fit the culture like antibodies discarding unwanted substances to keep a person healthy.
2. It converts some of them into loyal members because they are attracted to the strength and conviction of the leaders.
3. It fortifies the resolve of those who are already loyal to continue to improve and evangelize the culture.

Here are a few more important things to consider:

- The cultures that live deep within any organization will spill over into the customer and client experience. Low quality engineering standards, a crooked finance department, slow fulfillment, and deceitful sales practices all find their way to the end user, client, or point of sale.
- While a company's product has relative significance, how it's bought and sold is a result of the culture, and it will produce a "feeling" in the customer. That feeling is a big part of a "brand."
- A great culture will always (eventually) produce great strategy. This is because a great culture puts the best minds in an atmosphere where people make great decisions (Prudence), make fair policies (Justice), overcome difficult challenges (Fortitude), and keep morale positive and uplifting (Temperance).
- Salespeople keep the lights on, and the company funded. Treat them like an "officer on deck," understanding that a healthy sales culture has a disproportionate role in permeating the rest of the company culture.

When all of those things are happening with a culture, you simply won't let negative things grow and manifest. With a healthy culture, rarely do unfit people rise to high levels of authority. Bad ideas generally don't prevail, and pride is normally left at the door.

13

The Flow of Culture via Meetings, Email, Texts, and More

Although great decisions are made by using logic, reason, and data, when it comes to culture, those skills and tools are not as valuable as feelings, emotions, and intuition. Culture is more like music than it is the application of "policy" or "standards." Yet many leaders seem to look at culture as a task instead of an experience to craft and take in. Like music, which has certain powers over mood and behavior, the culture you're in greatly affects your thoughts, emotions, and feelings. Many leaders miss the fact that culture is transmitted via every interaction in their organization. It's transmitted via meetings, email, texts, stopping by a colleague's office, the rumor mill, dinners, and through social media.

So, a good question to ask when building a great culture is, "How do I want people to feel when they leave an interaction?" I imagine musicians ask themselves a similar question as they're writing, producing, or performing their song—"What do I want people to feel when they listen to this song? What memories will it evoke? How will it change their life?" To understand why I've chosen this metaphor—seeing how culture and music affect us similarly—here are five ways music impacts psychology, shared by Shahram Heshmat, PhD.[1] Music:

1. helps people cope with stress.
2. increases memory.
3. can relieve sadness or negative emotions even if the music is sad.
4. moves us motivationally and beyond.
5. alters time perception, making it move fast or slow.

If you build your culture with the metaphor of making it like great music, you will get these same five benefits, albeit in a different way. If culture is just a policy you have to enforce, you will fail. So, to have a culture that empowers the good and resolves what's bad, every person is required to "play the music" in every interaction.

Although great decisions are made by using logic, reason, and data, when it comes to culture, those skills and tools are not as valuable as feelings, emotions, and intuition.

We've already talked about the importance of marketing your culture by way of a culture statement (what it means to work here), continually repeating it in meetings, leading by example, etc., but culture is built and forged through every single interaction. When you meet someone at your door, take their call, or respond to a text, do you do it with a smile and kindness? Or are you under the impression that since your business is serious, you must personally take a serious tone? Granted, while there are times when someone can act inappropriately to the circumstance, the majority of interactions within most organizations do not demand a somber or overly serious demeanor. I have met generals, morticians, and professional coaches who use a kind, warm, and jovial tone in most settings despite the fact that, in battle, at a funeral, and during halftime, their tone shifts to fit the setting. Taking this into consideration, I have established a few guidelines to fortify a culture:

1. **Never send bad news in a text or email.**

   Communicate bad news via a live call or in person. It's of utmost importance to make sure your tone is as compassionate as is reasonable. The implementation of this as a cultural norm has reduced conflict in many organizations. It takes courage (Fortitude), so weak people often take the easier path, only to have it bite them in the ass later. Sometimes the subject deserves a rebuke, so it's not always butterflies and balloons, but even then, you want the tone to be precise and not more than necessary. Also, emails and texts are notoriously misread for tone. When a recipient gets upset without your ability to hear or see their reaction, they often stew to the point of creating even bigger problems for themselves and for you. When communicating is done properly, even very bad news can be digested in a way to prevent big problems in the first place. This is a great example of crushing vice, not necessarily by building virtue as much as supplementing a potential vice-filled subject with the good virtues you personally possess, such as compassion, thoughtful articulation, and patience.

2. **Cancel or shorten most of your meetings.**

   Replace them with one-on-one quick calls directed at the relevant parties. One of the biggest and most legitimate complaints in organizations is the overuse of meetings and inviting people not relevant to the circumstance. We have all been invited to in-person or virtual meetings with a group of people only to sit on our hands, twiddle our thumbs, or scroll social media. If you're ever in this situation, and it's in your scope to cancel or shorten the meeting, do it.

3. **Dump 90% of your Zoom meetings and just pick up the phone.** Before the global pandemic in 2020, Zoom was an obscure tool in the digital toolbox. Then, as the pandemic took hold, it quickly became a lifeline for businesses, schools, and families alike. Over-night, this once-niche application became the cornerstone of our daily interactions, a crutch we leaned on for meetings, catch-ups, and everything in between. But now, annoyed by the endless virtual backgrounds, forgotten muted microphones, spotty con-nections, and an overpriced subscription (all to be able to record a meeting that no one is likely to ever revisit), it's time to con-sider virtual meetings for what they provide and not more. They have merit and can enhance your communication portfolio, but only if used when necessary. Necessary times may include when: (1) there is a need to build, establish, and/or maintain a relation-ship at a level that requires face-to-face interaction (this is not a daily or weekly partner); (2) there is an exchange of visual data such as campaign designs; (3) you are sharing data that would be too clumsy to send ahead of time, follow along independently, or that you need to keep control over; or (4) you're hosting group interactions that become too clumsy with audio alone. Outside of those scenarios, the primary reason videoconferences are ineffec-tive is because they reduce efficiency. Sending an invite and the need to move to a specific location to take part in the meeting makes what could be a quick two-minute phone call more of an ordeal for all parties.

4. **Walk down the hall.**

   Even better than picking up the phone, when possible, is just walking down the hall to speak to your colleague. If you're afraid of interrupting someone, don't be. In the coming paragraphs I will demonstrate the value that interruptions can provide if they are within reason.

5. **When you meet for team building, don't spend too much time talking about the business. Take interest in the people, not only the work.**

   Unlike a business planning or review meeting, the true aim of team-building meetings should be to knit individuals into a tighter social fabric, enhancing trust, investment, and understanding. By focusing on the people who form the company, you'll improve collaboration and create a more connected, engaged environment. This doesn't mean endlessly rambling on about the upcoming game this weekend. It means considering the person behind the project or task or their relationship with it. How do they feel about it? What satisfaction do they get or what struggles are they managing? Boosting morale requires investing in the other person's experience.

6. **Use email primarily for the exchange of data or data-related information.**

   I have witnessed and officiated many conflicts that came from poorly worded emails. The common denominator was using email to convey messages that contained information that impacts emotions more than intellect. The strength of email comes from its ability to transfer data-oriented information and records, rather than being an effective tool for nuanced or emotional content. It provides clarity and reference, avoiding misinterpretation that can arise from more-complex discussions. By restricting email to data exchange, you'll encourage more in-person conversations and phone calls.

7. **Assume and communicate the best in others.**

   This is central to virtue, and it is a habit that can be built. When we get cynical, we destroy culture, build silos, and start turf wars. Starting any call or meeting with the assumption that the other person has good intentions builds trust. It may not end up being the case, but that's less common than not.

8. **Assume that your department serves the others.**

   No matter what department you're in, you serve the other departments. Administration "ministers" to others, which is why I stressed that when it comes to your sales team, treat them like they're an officer on deck. Every department is essential to the entire organization and giving others the benefit of the doubt increases the speed with which everyone can get things done, not to mention it increases job satisfaction.

INTERRUPTIVE CULTURE

My companies have what I call an "interruptive culture." We openly encourage quick interruptions that produce rapid answers and, therefore, fast results. Most organizations send meeting invites to one or several people days in advance for answers to questions that could be concluded in 90 seconds via a phone call or by walking down the hall. While our competition waits until Tuesday to get an answer to their client, we get it within minutes. Since an answer or conclusion is likely to be needed by more than just one person in order to make changes or get answers to key people, including clients, there's a domino effect when someone has a question that needs answering.

At first, this is difficult for new team members to grasp. It almost seems disrespectful when they first experience it, but once they catch on, they see the benefits for themselves. The interruptive culture has another very important benefit—it's used as a teaching opportunity in order to develop and mentor people rapidly. Ironically, by instituting an interruptive culture, you will experience fewer interruptions (and fewer unnecessary scheduled meetings) than non-interruptive cultures because an interruptive culture creates a problem-solving workforce of Giants.

Here's the thing most leaders miss: people over-interrupt because they're being micromanaged or because they don't know how to make decisions on their own. This makes them afraid to act independently. In the case of micromanagement, you'll hear things like, "I wanted to make this decision, but I can't because whenever I make a decision, my boss asks why I didn't run that by him first. So now, I'm going to run everything by him, so I don't get in trouble."

If you have people on your team who are poor decision-makers, you have only two choices: train them to make better decisions or remove them from the role. When a person interrupts, I'll say, "*First, I want you to state your question or problem in one sentence if you can. If you need a second sentence, fine, but please keep it as concise as possible. Then, second, after you tell me your question, challenge, or problem, I want you to tell me what you think are the top three solutions. Finally, explain which one of those three solutions you favor, and why.*"

This filtering process is what creates an empowered workforce, and interruptions are a *tremendous* training ground for the kind of culture you need to succeed. This process usually makes the answers so obvious that the next time, they decide not to ask in the first place. That is to say, they decide for themselves. Anecdotally, I'd say nine out of ten times, your people will solve the problem without interrupting. In the event that they still interrupt, you now have the opportunity to witness how they frame the problem as well as how and what solutions they choose. If they are good at what they do, you will likely just say, "I agree, well done." If they still keep coming in because they can't either frame proper challenges, make good decisions, or take action, then you need to figure out why. It could be that you or someone else is overmanaging them and thus creating fear. Also, it could be that they are not qualified, either permanently (untrainable) or temporarily (undertrained).

Instead of brushing them off, you must properly train them. Now that you know how they think in error, you need to teach them to think properly. If they can learn to think properly, they can be retained. Eventually, they will come to you with three solid solutions, and they will favor the best one. Over time, they will interrupt less and produce more. However, if they can't grasp this concept, they can't stay in the role. Why? Reflecting back on chapter 1, it's because they're not demonstrating Prudence, the foundational virtue. Remember, wisdom is the ability to define the top three solutions and pick their favorite one—this perfectly demonstrates Prudence, the mastery of decision-making. As a result, they cannot possess Justice, Fortitude, and Temperance, as Prudence is the bedrock for all others.

People who lack Prudence push blame on others because, as I also mentioned in chapter 1, Prudence requires "desiring what is good, knowing what is true, and pursuing what is good." People who fail here fight incredibly hard to preserve their egos. So, they blame others for their own shortcomings. In turn, they will commonly try to cover the fact that they're unable to make decisions by lashing out aggressively. Also, they generally have no ability to endure. An interruptive culture is a built-in way to identify these traits and characteristics within the various teams, therefore eliminating destructive behaviors and elevating people accordingly.

Keep in mind that you can't give what you don't have. Be certain to work on yourself while leading others. If your pride is unbridled, you may hear someone solve a problem coherently but decide to feed your ego by nitpicking at their solution. When you do this, you strip their creativity and confidence, and, what's worse, you become perceived as a dictator.

As a leader, you must epitomize the culture you've instilled. Does this mean you can't falter or have a bad day? Not at all, which is why you should have a cultural statement and people on your team who know that grace must be given when it's due. Simultaneously, if and when someone begins demonstrating destructive behaviors or dictator-like actions, their due must also be given to them. Even after doing so much work to instill a truly beautiful, dare I say transcendent, culture, bad apples can emerge. Often, they are so crafty that some people don't realize their presence, or so brazen that others are too afraid to step up and guard the culture. As the leader, it's your job to have the courage, conviction, confidence, and compassion to stop people who don't fit the culture in their tracks. Thankfully, they're easy to track down because, as the title of this chapter suggests, their grasp of the culture is transmitted via every interaction.

GIANT TAKEAWAYS

Culture is transmitted via every interaction in an organization, via meetings, email, texts, stopping by a colleague's office, the rumor mill, dinners, and through social media. How do you want people to feel when they leave an interaction? Taking that question into consideration, here are the guidelines to fortify a culture:

1. Never send bad news in a text or email.
2. Cancel or shorten most of your meetings.
3. Dump 90% of your Zoom meetings and just pick up the phone.
4. Walk down the hall.
5. When you meet for team building, don't spend too much time talking about the business. Take interest in the people, not only the work.
6. Use email primarily for the exchange of data or data-related information.
7. Assume and communicate the best in others.
8. Assume that your department serves the others.

Utilize the "interruptive culture," which is to openly encourage quick interruptions that produce rapid answers and, therefore, fast results. Interruptions are a *tremendous* training ground for the kind of culture you need to succeed. But if someone is interrupting too much—that is to say, they're not being prudent—train them in the way I offered to become adept at decision-making. Then, you'll have taught them to think for themselves while simultaneously making them, and your organization, more efficient.

Watch out for those that will destroy a good culture with their own egos, agendas, and ideas. While many are so crafty that people don't realize their presence, others are so brazen that people are too afraid to step up and guard the culture. Either way, it's your job to notice the signs before and while they're happening.

14

When All Else Fails . . .

'm going to let you in on a couple secrets that I hinted at in the Introduction. When I first started writing this book, I quipped to a few colleagues that my working title was *Punch a Bully in the Face.* I went with this idea, as a not-so-serious working title, because it's relevant, eye-grabbing, and exciting. In the same not-so-serious way, I pitched the title to a few people who, to my surprise, loved it. Understanding that it's clearly metaphorical, they were relieved to finally hear someone speaking about the importance of standing your ground. But as happens often in the process of writing, when I began to organize the content, a more accurate and serious title, theme, and message emerged.

As I'm sure you've noted, the book you're reading aims to support you in becoming an extraordinary leader, which ultimately comes through the mastery of self and then of influence, not force. However, to be a Giant, you must have the ability to shut down problematic people or situations that place your company, culture, and success in jeopardy. Giants have self-agency and the confidence to respond. Giants have the ability to be ferocious despite being docile in practice. They know that forces exist that will, either intentionally or unintentionally, try to destroy your success. Armed with that knowledge, they find ways to navigate all situations gracefully and peacefully unless all options are exhausted. Then, only if need be, they fight fairly and without complaining. Nanos see themselves as victims—they take normal behaviors from others and misperceive them as bully-like actions. This causes them to fight often, and always unfairly. Whereas in the rare instance when someone is a bully, a Giant's words are few, but their actions are big. That is what I mean when I say, "punch a bully," and I must add, the full insight is this: "When all else fails, *sometimes*, you have to punch a bully in the face" (metaphorically, obviously, in the workplace).

Other than the obvious, some key words may stand out to you, like *sometimes* or *when all else fails*. I very intentionally say *sometimes* because not all people who are bullying others would respond well to a forceful wake-up call. For some, this could make them even more brazen. The goal of a Giant is to shut down the problem, not to go to war. So, the most measured, least confrontational approach is always the first line of action. Thankfully, most people who've stepped out of line will have the rapid, humble self-reflection that maybe, just maybe, they've done something to deserve it. Therefore, a measured approach is wise to prevent elevating situations. But when it's time to go toe-to-toe, Giants know how to use their power.

To be in a place where you can consider this as an option requires you to have established a sense of organizational safety and a healthy culture. Nine out of ten times, there's likely another solution, but sometimes you must decide to use power instead of influence. In leadership, there are two ways to get things done and motivate people:

1. Through influence: soft power.
2. Through directives or force: hard power.

Influence involves persuading and inspiring others to take action because they genuinely want to or because they share the same values and goals as you. In business, this most directly happens by way of the culture in place. On the other hand, hard power involves the use of authority or punishments to induce action. It's a more direct approach, and an effective leader knows how to use a combination of both, depending on the situation and desired outcomes. In my observation and experience, there is a 99% to 1% soft to hard power ratio. So, while a punchy title would have surely turned a few heads and raised some eyebrows, the true message of this book is that leadership success hinges on utilizing soft power with savvy and skill, but you must have the empathy and wisdom to provide appropriate doses of hard power when needed. The mastery of influence is the mission of a Giant, and the misuse of force is the fatal error of a weakling. So, when I say that it's only appropriate to punch a bully "when all else fails," I'm strictly speaking to Giants and Leaders of Giants.

Furthermore, the "all else" refers to everything you've read up until this point. You began this book with the Cardinal Virtues and how they should guide and direct all of your professional and personal actions. You next learned about the three steps of decision-making, which are to "desire what is good, know what is real, and do what is good." Building upon Prudence and the other three virtues, you read about the Transcendentals, which supported you to write a cultural statement that sets forth the expectations of behaviors for everyone in your organization. Then, to truly be a Giant, you've begun to ensure that everyone guards the culture, helping people to see that great decisions are made by using logic, reason, and data, but when it comes to culture, those skills and tools are not as valuable as feelings, emotions, and intuition.

Only when you've implemented all of these things within your own life and then for those you lead, if someone slips through the cracks, sometimes you have to let them eat a metaphorical knuckle sandwich if that's what they're cooking up for themselves. It's not preferable, and it's almost always best to find another solution, but to be a Giant, you have to do what's necessary. Make no mistake—only a true Giant can even consider this as a possible leadership strategy. A Giant would never punch up at senior leadership, nor punch down on subordinates without Prudence and Justice in his or her corner. Giants like you are considerate when exercising power.

NOPE, THAT'S NOT HAPPENING HERE

Bullies usually pick fights they know they can win, and so they target weaker people. This happens with dictators and world leaders, and it happens in most playgrounds, schoolyards, and offices everywhere. Throughout my own life, I've occasionally experienced this in childhood, athletics, and business. I'll never forget the day I encountered the town bully as a youngster. It was a typical summer day, and my brother and I had stopped at the local store for some treats, our bikes propped against the wall outside. My brother, having finished his treat before I had finished mine, was already out of the store. That's when the bully, unaware that I was inside, decided to corner my younger brother. His voice carried through the open door. "Do you want to get hit?" In a heartbeat, I stepped outside to defend my brother. "Do *you* want to get hit?" I said, throwing his threat back at him, my voice steady. The bully, picking on someone five years younger than he, was taken aback by my sudden appearance and challenge. He did the only thing he could—pedaled away as fast as he could, his perceived power deflating like a punctured tire. But this story doesn't end there. Two years later, he wrangled up a gang of about 10 guys his age and older, all of them older and larger than me. Without saying a word, he walked up and decked me.

That's just the way bullies are. They can't handle anything that's not a sure victory. Bullies are the weakest kind of people, not only physically and mentally, but almost always emotionally. They are unstable and mostly void of virtue. Ultimately, they're egocentric, so their whole purpose is to look powerful and build self-esteem, yet they are very easily offended, and they have a double standard for everyone. They expect to be treated a certain way, with certain privileges, and a certain respect that, mind you, they don't provide anyone else—unless they're trying to get something from that person. Narcissism and bullying are quite often paired like fire and fuel.

You will have negative forces in your organization that try to defeat it with their own agendas. At some point, a person on your team will threaten you or others, creating discord via their go-to vices like gossip or backstabbing. Once, a team member demanded he be paid what somebody else (who was outperforming him by five times) was getting paid even though he didn't have a legitimate reason to merit it. He was already being paid very well yet declared that he was upset and demanded a bigger bonus. He made a veiled threat to make waves with other team members and went on to say that his colleague's larger bonus was not fair. This is how I responded: I said, "You are right—it is not fair. You have been overpaid for a long time. Remember when I generously increased your sales commission to provide stability when you lost your largest client? That wasn't required, nor part of your contract. That was me being generous, not fair, to help you through a disappointing time. If we really want to use fairness as our guide on your compensation, then you should return half of what you've earned. So, I recommend you find a different justification for your desire for a larger bonus because the fairness argument will set you back."

If you give somebody something for nothing,
they're going to want even more for less.

This principle is sadly true because good people can be corrupted by unmerited benefits. For that reason, many capable people decline entitlements they can technically receive according to classification but that don't fit their situation. These good people want to earn what they have, not get a handout. That is not to say others who are truly in need should not accept them. In leadership, there are times when it is important to provide special treatment to people who may not merit it in the exact moment but who have demonstrated a certain level of loyalty or dependability. There is a subjective space in which leaders apply their generosity, and in doing so, build a strong culture. If a person is not virtuous, this approach can backfire, but it is still worth risking in most situations.

When it goes wrong, subtle poor behavior can rear its head. This can happen in the form of passive-aggression or other forms of subtle intellectual domination and control. Most leaders fall for these manipulations, not realizing they have been controlled or pushed around—for example, when, out of laziness, somebody tells you they can't get their job done. Often, this type of person pits two good things against each other like, "I'd be the top salesperson, but I'm a family man." All experienced leaders have had, at one time or another, someone come to them with a litany of reasons why they couldn't do their job. Giants listen to these complaints with an open mind to determine what truth may be in them, but the passive-aggressive, subtly controlling person does not bring legitimate complaints to the table. They spew blame and self-justification. Ironically, if they spent the same amount of time working as they did to compile all their excuses, they would have likely solved their problems.

Using hard power to shake them out of their stupor is wise. You may say something like, "You're doing a good job convincing me that you can't do your job. I need you to know that, if you succeed, you will have talked yourself out of working here. I'd need to replace you because there's no way I can keep you in the role if you continue to tell me that you are not able to get it done. Carry on if you'd like, or instead, you can tell me what it will take for you to get the job done in a more productive manner."

These techniques can sound like you're Mr. Tough Guy or some hotshot leader who won't be pushed around. But if you're reading this the right way, you know hard power techniques should be very rarely used and only for the benefit of all parties. If you run your business with routine hard power tactics, you're going to fail, quickly and catastrophically. Strive to treat everyone with mercy and with a spirit of generosity. Mastering influence will allow you to stay in more equanimous styles of leadership, which is what will sustain your success. But when somebody to whom you give something for nothing starts to cry foul or plays victim, it's important to stay keen to the idea that they may be trying to control you. In that instance, you must recognize that if you give them more for even less effort, they will eventually become dissatisfied with everything. Then, it's time to clearly convey, "Nope, that's not happening here," in ways that demonstrate your authority.

VIRTUE IS A TYRANT'S KRYPTONITE

A lie is not miscommunication; it's anti-communication. There is no Prudence in a lie. As a result, there's no Justice, Temperance, or Fortitude in a lie either. When a person lies to you, or they flatter you to get something, to some degree they're saying to you, "I have little respect for you. You're a thing to me. You're merely a tool, an object for me to use, not a subject for me to explore, learn to love, and find richness therein. No, you are something for me to try to dominate and overpower with my own desires." Such behavior makes a genuine relationship impossible and a losing culture inevitable. In a workplace context, when dealing with an out-of-hand employee, this manipulative behavior often begins with flattery, gossip, or lies. These tactics are their primary tools, and threats usually come only after this fails. It's vital to be vigilant and recognize these signs as they indicate the deepest lack of respect possible.

Interestingly, tyrants only respect those they can't dominate and, sometimes, standing up to them can earn their respect or even, paradoxically, their liking. Some of the most loyal people I've ever known were at one time exhibiting destructive behaviors. Standing up to them and making it clear their agendas held no weight and carried no merit often worked well. The best of them saw the error of their ways, but it only came from facing someone stronger than them. Loyalty in business is naturally hard to come by, and oftentimes, it happens by going into battle alongside or against someone. The only way to survive these moments is to be equipped with the training and techniques required to succeed.

Being virtuous is not only your best means of protection but also of winning. Once you exercise the muscles required to be a Giant, you'll be far less susceptible to being targeted by nanos, tyrants, and the like. It'll still likely happen in some form or another, so be vigilant in the face of someone who's not up to creating something good, true, or beautiful. Giants need to know that you'll stand your ground, because even Giants want to be protected too.

Standing up for the greater good
makes decisions simpler.

EFFECTIVE LEADERSHIP DEPENDS ON INFLUENCE

Here's a fact: Giants don't spend too much time talking about bullies, but they know they exist. It's like the Transcendentals; they lose their magic by being overexplained. Calling someone a bully for the sake of making yourself sound or look more powerful or victimized is a classic nano move. A Giant doesn't often label people bullies. When faced with one, he or she simply responds appropriately and decisively. It's all in a day's work, without fanfare, for a true Giant. As a result, there are very few people who try to bully a Giant.

Giants demonstrate enough strength and have so many decisive victories that their adversaries think twice. Giants demonstrate their strength, no surprise, via Prudence, Justice, Fortitude, Temperance, and humility. They believe in what is good and true, creating unquestionable beauty in the world. Because these are signs of strength, they attract more followers than enemies. It's uncommon for someone to confront a strong individual directly. They typically opt for indirect methods, like anonymous attacks through social media or negative reviews. Such tactics allow them to gather support against you without facing you directly. This approach stems from audacity, a vice that contradicts Prudence. Audacity involves overestimating one's own abilities, like facing a hungry lion, thinking you can win. It's a trait rooted in pride, leading people to believe they can succeed in situations where they're clearly underdeveloped.

In leadership, effectiveness depends on influence. If you're going to lead, you have to influence people. If you're going to sell, you have to influence people. If you're in entertainment, you're going to have an influence on people. The bigger your organization gets and the more you advance your role, the greater potential you have to influence others. This is true even if you don't hold a formal position of authority. True leadership is not synonymous with a title. You might lead effectively without any official appointment.

As you aim to lead Giants, you first need to master yourself and then master influence. Hard power does not mean being a hard-ass. When dealing with the extensive and legitimate stressors of founding, leading, and scaling a company, some people default to that approach, but that's the lazy option. Sure, it may feel good to blow off steam on a team that's underdeveloped or underdelivering, but all that does is strip you of any credibility—and it's a surefire way to completely bankrupt your influence.

Instead, lead with gracefulness, without hesitating to stand your ground when you absolutely must. When that kind of culture is in place, dealing with adversaries isn't going to happen often. But when it does, now you know exactly what to do.

Power doesn't mean influence, but influence always brings power.

GIANT TAKEAWAYS

Becoming an extraordinary leader ultimately comes through the mastery of influence and not force. However, to be a Giant, you must have the ability to shut down problematic people or situations that place your company, culture, and success in jeopardy. Since the goal of a Giant is to shut down problems, not to go to war, the most measured, least confrontational approach is always the first line of action. But when it's time to go toe-to-toe, Giants know how to use power. In leadership, there are two ways to get things done and motivate people:

1. Through influence: soft power.
2. Through directives or force: hard power.

The true message of this book is that leadership success hinges on utilizing soft power with savvy and skill, but you must have the empathy and wisdom to provide appropriate doses of hard power when needed. The mastery of influence is the mission of a Giant, and the misuse of force is the fatal error of a weakling. A Giant would never punch up at senior leadership or punch down on subordinates without Prudence and Justice in his corner. Giants are considerate when exercising power. In leadership, effectiveness depends on influence.

SECTION 3
Think Like a Criminal

A detective who's solving a crime must think like a criminal. An attorney who's questioning somebody on the stand should know everything their subject could say in response to every question, including each excuse they might make for their behaviors. Similarly, police officers often laugh about the unoriginal excuses they hear when somebody gets a ticket. As humans, we all make the same types of self-justifications, yet we think we're being original. Great leaders need to learn to think like excuse-makers, which can be difficult if they personally aren't prone to making excuses. Doing this allows leaders to see patterns, which I will discuss in chapter 16, regarding people who exhibit excuse-making tendencies, controlling behaviors such as passive-aggression, or egocentric motives.

"Thinking like a criminal" might sound cynical or skeptical. It could be perceived as simply seeing the worst in others, but that's not the point. It's about helping people, not accusing them. It's not about assuming the worst in people. Instead, it's about knowing that even the best people can have bad behaviors. Really, it's about insurance. When people respect your intuition and ability to judge them accurately and fairly, they are less inclined to deceive you. It's influence armor. You may occasionally have some people who try, but if they know you have a fine-tuned BS detector, they will think twice. Additionally, when you admit mistakes and faults of your own, you build trust with others, which allows you to be more direct with them if you detect they are acting disingenuously. Humility is living with the knowledge that you're not above them because everyone has the same human nature—how we act is what makes all the difference when the time comes to confront someone.

Giants use data to help their teams reduce excuses and bad behaviors. As you will see in chapter 17, the more you can use data to create objective standards of performance, the more you empower your team members to get results. Leading with data as an aid helps raise the bar for all team members, so this section is important for overall performance and culture. It also puts guardrails up for the more extreme situations that bad actors create in organizational health. But make no mistake, the use of data will not solve all your leadership woes. You will always have subjective areas that require strong intuition based on experience.

Because influence is more powerful when it's unspoken and subtle, Giants carry a presence that commands a certain respect. It's more about savvy, doing things with a wink and a smile. It's about winning someone over whenever possible. In the presence of someone who's prone to excuse-making, a Giant says things like, "I get where you are right now. I've been there, so I understand." This demonstrates that you do or have struggled the same as they do. Leaning into your empathetic side, they will see you have their own benefit in mind. Thinking like a criminal is done from a place of compassion and understanding, doing so to prevent bad behaviors or help them overcome a bad behavior if it takes place. If you confront an excuse-maker with force or hard power, you'll likely just make them angry and give fuel to their delusions.

A clear difference between a Giant and a nano is that the Giant knows the difference between an excuse and a reason. The nano is so convinced by their excuses they think they're actually convincing others. One of the greatest ways to help somebody if they make an excuse is to repeat it back to them as a question. So, if somebody says something like, "I'm late because of traffic," and you knew there was no traffic, simply say, "Because of traffic?" They now have to answer their own objection because you put it in the form of a question. A person who was truly late due to traffic will usually just say, "Yes, it was horrible." An excuse-maker might fess up and admit their error, but often they will use many more words to make their lie seem more believable.

When thinking like a criminal, you'll ask, "What has my experience taught me about working with somebody in sales, in finance, or somebody who provides an expense report? What have I learned from working with others that I have also observed about myself when it comes to the desire to make excuses?" Being mindful, when you communicate with them, you're going to get ahead of all of these excuses because you begin to identify the patterns that precede excuses. The difference between a Giant and a nano is not in the temptation to make excuses, it's whether or not you act on them. That allows you to be aware of likely excuses. You'll let them know they might be tempted to say or do something. By setting things up ahead of time, you protect them from themselves.

Preventative measures can be used to ensure future performances. For example, to prepare a candidate for a possible promotion, you can get ahead of excuses that could come up after they are promoted. I have asked candidates to reflect on whether to accept a promotion by asking them to look at it this way. A flight student has a right to pursue becoming or not becoming a pilot, but nobody has the right to be a bad pilot. Likewise, a medical student has the right to become a doctor or not, but no one has a right to be a bad doctor. Before I offer someone a position, I want them to know what the responsibility entails and that a certain level of commitment is required. Once I do that, they will accept the promotion with clear expectations about future responsibilities and results. Setting this expectation preemptively addresses the potential to make unvirtuous decisions. Thinking like this, though it may sound pessimistic, is rooted in compassion and understanding of human nature. You should get ahead of potential issues because you care. Initially, it is easier to ignore potential problems, but it's a better idea to help shift that person away from vice and into greater virtue.

Creating high expectations is not the same as surrounding yourself with yes-men. It should not be your aim to eliminate future conflict when setting expectations, because it is important to have healthy conflict in your organization. Assuming that anyone who disagrees with you is some-how "bad" for the culture or not up for a promotion is a mistake. Be careful not to think you should get "full consensus" on all issues, therefore exposing anyone who disagrees with you as nefarious. That would weaken your team and create a one-dimensional environment. It would amplify the leader's ego and reduce problem-solving capabilities. Healthy conflict and runaway ego are not the same. In this section you will learn to motivate, inspire, retain, and develop leaders to the next level by gaining certain insights regarding human nature. As always, see where you need to improve on a personal level before you look only at the improvements your team must make.

15

The Three Most Powerful Motivators Are Love, Self-Justification, and Fear, in That Order

DON'T CRASH INTO FLOATING ROCKS

Many years ago, I had a colleague who was also a friend. One of the perks of his job was taking breaks with me to visit my lake house. We would eat together, go for an occasional midday ski, and then return to the office. Due to this routine, I let him take my boat out from time to time. There was a tricky part of the lake where straying from the usual path could easily lead to hitting a rock with the boat's propeller. All these areas were clearly marked, and because I personally showed him where they were, he was in a small club of people whom I let drive the boat on this particular lake.

One day, he wanted to take the boat out by himself. I reminded him again to stay on the path. When he returned, the boat was clearly limping. He had absolutely, without question, hit a rock. I asked him what happened, and before I even finished, he said, "I didn't go off the path. I stayed right where I was supposed to." I said, "You stayed on the path?" To which he clarified, "Yes, but there was a *floating rock*." To this day I haven't seen or heard of floating rocks, yet that was his excuse for the damage to the boat. Sensing his obvious embarrassment, I put him at ease, and in a comical, albeit bewildered, way, I asked, "A floating rock? It sounds more like you went off the path and hit a regular rock." Instead of further justifying himself, he immediately accepted responsibility for straying from the path.

So, what made him come to the place of admitting what he had done? I believe it was due to the fact that I put him at ease by not getting angry or making him feel stupid for his excuse. If I had doubled down or attacked him, I'd not only have lost a boat propeller that day but also a friend. You must think in terms of your own tendency for self-justification so you can respond with curiosity and empathy when others try to use excuses instead of reasons. The more you learn to respond in these ways, the more you help people become successful. People will remain motivated when they know you won't attack them personally for a personal or professional failing. However, it's your responsibility to ensure things are done with integrity.

When people are late for no good reason, such as spending time on social media or sleeping in, they usually don't admit it. I've polled thousands of people on what excuse they use instead of admitting their actual fault and 99.9% of them say the same thing: traffic. Why? Because traffic is difficult to argue against and not their fault. Most people need to justify their bad behaviors because admitting them pierces their ego too much. Self-justification is incredibly powerful. As a leader, you must know this and head it off at the pass. Preemptive measures are the best.

I recently had somebody ask me for a big personal loan. He gave me some great terms, a "guaranteed" good return on investment, and other assurances people tend to make in this kind of situation. Mind you, this loan was not to help his impoverished mother or to get out of a hard place himself. This loan was a way for him to make a lot of money by using my money without personal financial risk on his end. I agreed, but only after I made myself very, very clear. I told him, "If we do this, here's what's going to happen on the day the loan is due. If this is not acceptable, then don't take the loan. On the due date, you are going to pay me back in full, with *all* of the interest that you said. Additionally, here are some conversations that are not going to happen. 'Oh, I know I said I was going to pay you, but now I have a hard life circumstance.' Or 'My investment didn't work out!' Or 'Are you really telling me that I'd have to mortgage my house to pay you back?'"

Thinking like a criminal is about forecasting self-justifications in those you lead, but doing so charitably. Having learned many times how that kind of loan usually goes sideways, I made him promise that no matter what the circumstances were, no matter how the investment turned out, he could pay me back on that agreed-upon day, no matter what, with zero exceptions. He promised, and the transaction went off without a hitch. Those standards made the loan work because even though his investment didn't go as planned, he had every intention to pay it back.

Setting forth standards of behavior and holding strong boundaries is useful when leading. Self-justification is a cancer that has and continues to erode all kinds of culture along with personal, romantic, and professional relationships. Self-justification happens because someone doesn't feel the confidence to take accountability or accept the pain of being held accountable when it's deserved. As a leader, proactive preventative measures blended with reactive empathetic approaches reduce the frequency and depth of self-justification in those you lead.

SELF-JUSTIFICATION IS SANDWICHED BETWEEN LOVE AND FEAR

People will do anything for love because it is the greatest of all motivators. Remarkable acts of love can appear extreme, but they're also admired, leading those who aren't experiencing love to at least think, *I'd love to be loved that much*. Love is the most powerful motivator because it is sacrificial, and that gives it a unique strength.

On the other side, fear is another strong motivator that can drive people to act unpredictably. Relying solely on fear results in failure, burnout, fatigue, and a breakdown of good health and balanced living. Occasional fear, balanced with courage, can lead to better outcomes and consistency. In rare cases, fear can lead to positive actions, but it's not a reliable or healthy driving force long term.

As highlighted earlier, the most dangerous motivator is self-justification because it's fueled by pride. Self-justification exists somewhere between love and fear and it's so powerful that it can make you see floating rocks. Motivation from fear comes from a perceived need for self-preservation, but self-justification is an entirely different beast. The grave danger with pride is that it comes with blindness, so you can't tell when you have it. When motivated by pride (i.e., self-justification), you're capable of giving yourself a pass on behaviors you wouldn't normally accept from anyone else. Human beings are capable of justifying pretty much anything, as long as it benefits them, at least in the short term.

Self-justification is a battle between how we perceive ourselves and who we actually are.

Feeling the need to self-justify often comes from a need to be right, predicated on a fear of being perceived as wrong, weak, or inept. No truly confident person would ever need to justify their actions because if and when they make a genuine mistake, they will immediately have the humility to admit it, learn from it, and move on. The problem is that most of us are not fully confident, even if we are confident most of the time.

Excuses cause fissures in relationships, creating separation between the excuse-maker and the very people that likely want what's best for them. To be motivated by a need to be right will never, ever create a winning culture. Love, not fear or insecurity, is what gives strength to a Giant and fuels the heart of a champion.

HOT BUTTONS VS. DEEP DESIRES

When I was younger, a well-known motivational speaker suggested motivating people by identifying their "hot buttons"—essentially, triggering what satiates their surface-level desires. For instance, they might say buying a new TV or taking a vacation would make them feel better. His idea was to link their sales performance to these desires: "Sell more, and you'll earn enough to buy that thing you want." The strategy included visualizing their goal, like putting a picture of it on their mirror, to constantly remind them. Does this method make an impact? Possibly, to an extent. However, if it were that simple, anyone who puts a picture of a Ferrari on their mirror would have an exotic car in their driveway six months later.

This idea comes and goes in various forms of pop culture. Years ago, the best-selling book *The Secret* emphasized sending messages to the universe regarding desires. The book's appeal was that it was easy. The author suggests that sending a message to the "universe" will get the "universe" to conspire on your behalf. On a side note, I find it interesting how people who discard faith in God have faith in a nameless, nonpersonal universe, claiming it hears you and can give you cool things. That requires much more faith than faith in God. You can't simply tell the universe that you want a new bike, wish for your bills to disappear, and then expect a new bike along with checks to arrive in the mail. Yet, this is what the movie adaptation of *The Secret* suggests. Giants understand motivation and desire at a deeper level.

A person who doesn't think past owning a Ferrari is likely to be a one-hit wonder. He is also very easy prey to silly ideas like those in *The Secret*. His short-term motivation may serve him for a short period of time, but not much longer. A high-minded person who wants to become a better person will be committed to greater things and will endure hardships with grace, keeping him engaged when others quit. He will also be less influenced by superficial advice. Greatness needs a stage, which is why Giants use problems and challenges to exercise their talents. "I can be my best self by making all my calls because that's going to strengthen me. And, as a result, I will become more of who I was meant to be." This isn't to say that Giants don't own nice things like Ferraris. But someone motivated solely by surface-level desires like that falls into the common pattern of going from one Ferrari to the next, ad infinitum.

A person who is motivated by self-justification or fear, which usually manifests as insecurity, may buy a Ferrari to make others think he is great. Why? Because he identifies his self-worth with what he wants. On the other hand, someone who becomes great by building something great does not need anything external to affirm himself. A person motivated by love is more apt to accomplish great things. Lovers are irreplaceable, magnetic, and attractive. They not only win in business, but they win in life. As I said previously, if you master the cabinet business, you can stay in the cabinet business and be relatively successful. If you master yourself, you can go anywhere and have most anything because you will have more to give.

WHAT SUCCESSFUL PEOPLE TALK ABOUT BUT OTHERS DON'T

Successful leaders talk about different things than leaders who fail. Successful people talk about good ideas, concepts, the culture they're building, outcomes that their products produce (which is very different than the product itself), and the like. Entrepreneurs who fail usually talk about new technologies, products, or an invention. No doubt these topics are also important to people who succeed but they are a means to an end, not the end itself. Unsuccessful leaders also gossip and talk about petty issues. What's interesting to a Giant is the problem they're solving, not the invention they're making. That's not a subtle difference. People who fail often get so committed to their "inventions" or their own ideas that they fail to see the big picture, which is the solution the invention provides. When that happens, they begin defending their ideas and get trapped in narrow-minded thinking, which stymies creativity and growth. Successful people don't really care about how something is solved, as long as it is solved (although there are limits because Giants know that the ends don't justify the means).

"DON'T YOU SEE MY CAR!?"

One of the greatest dangers of self-justification is that it runs against our desired outcomes. If you want to be respected but you self-justify, you will fail to earn respect. This happens in daily, subtle interactions, including the following anecdote.

I absolutely love my local drive-thru dry cleaner. I can drop off my laundry with ease. I simply drive up and they take it away with a smile. The young employees are always so upbeat and full of energy. Most are in college and even the more senior workers are full of passion. One day, I was in the drive-thru, and the line wasn't moving because of someone ahead of the rest of us, which was very unusual. One of the young ladies who worked there was outside talking to a man sitting in his car in line, and it was taking forever. I had no choice but to get out of my car and walk in, which was as awkward as leaving your car in a McDonald's drive-thru.

As I passed this guy in his brand-new Mercedes, I saw him pointing and yelling at the young lady, who was barely 20, and he was in his 40s. He was shouting, "When I demand something, I expect to get it. I'm the type of man who, if I have an expectation, it's met."

I walked in and said to another employee, "Your coworker's having a tough time out there, isn't she?"

She replied, "You have no idea. He was berating me for the last 10 minutes, so she took over."

Hearing this, I headed outside. I confronted him, saying, "I see you're a very important man," and before I could say anything further, he said, "I am important. Don't you see my car!?"

Laughing inside but seeing the kind of person we were dealing with, I replied, "Brother, having 10 of those cars doesn't make you important. Why don't you leave her alone?"

He did, but not without repeating, "You must not see my car. Look at my car. You know I'm important."

The young lady told me he claimed he dropped off his *entire* wardrobe two days ago and was promised it back the same day. In reality, he dropped off only a few items the day before. He was refusing to pay for it and set up a false scenario, all in an unconscious attempt to validate his importance.

In the end, this guy wanted respect, but he went about it entirely wrong, and he was disrespected. Theologians tell us that no matter what sin a person commits, they do it because they are seeking something good, even if the means are misguided. For example, some drug users seek peace by escaping mental or emotional pain. This guy desired something good, which was respect, but he went about it the wrong way.

This is why having empathy for people who are self-justifying is a good idea. Being a leader requires having the ability to identify self-justification in real time, responding decisively in ways that shift people out of vice and into virtue. In most instances, this requires understanding and empathy, both of which require strength. A great way to start is to identify your own self-justifications.

GIANT TAKEAWAYS

- Influencing others by your own lived example of not being an excuse-maker will make you extremely magnetic.
- Self-justification is a cancer that has and continues to erode all kinds of culture, and thus, personal, romantic, and professional relationships suffer greatly as a result.
- Fear is an unsustainable motivator.
- Feeling the need to self-justify often comes from a need to be right, predicated on a fear of being perceived as wrong, weak, or inept. Confident people don't need to justify their actions because if and when they make a genuine mistake, they will immediately have the humility to admit it, learn from it, and move on.
- A person who becomes great by building something great does not need anything external to affirm himself.
- Giants talk about ideas and purposes. They don't gossip and get fixated on the means versus the end.
- If you hurt someone or make a mistake, being motivated by love, you'll seek immediate reconciliation.
- No matter what wrong a person commits, they do it because they are seeking something good, even if the means are misguided. This is why having empathy for the accused is a good idea.
- Motivating people because you genuinely love them is the epitome of strength—a testament to the power of love in shaping a better world.

Ask yourself these questions, and write down your responses to review later:

1. How well do I own up to my mistakes and learn from them?
2. In which areas do I have a sense of lack in my life? How does that negatively affect me and others?
3. Am I more prone to talk about big ideas or about other people?

16

Most People Would Rather Be Right to Their Own Demise Than Wrong to Their Own Prosperity

There are 16 different personality types according to most experts. Where people fall short in application when it comes to these personality types is by neglecting the significance of virtue and vice. Rather than take on the arduous task of analyzing all 16 personality types, we will focus on three vice versus virtue types that stand out regardless of temperament or personality.

The first is the Team Player (TP). The TP is a high-virtue, low-vice person who is interested in the best outcome for the company. He is well informed, humble, and interested. The second is the Ambitious Team Player (ATP). He is torn between what is best for the company and what is best for himself. He is a political creature who has a blend of virtuous behaviors and vice-oriented weak moments. Therefore, in the event

215

that a project comes into play that could advance his career, he is smart enough to say things like, "You seem to have a lot on your plate, so I'd be happy to take this responsibility for you," even though this has nothing to do with helping the other party. Yet, on other occasions he does do things in a selfless manner. The third personality is the Egotistical Individual Player (EIP). He has almost no interest in what is good for the team unless it serves him. He has very low virtue and operates mostly from a vice-oriented perspective. He is a person with either full-blown narcissism or heavy narcissistic tendencies.

The EIP enters a meeting with one thing on his mind: stroking his ego. His job and his colleagues are there to serve his self-esteem. He demands respect but is not willing to earn it. He finds those who disagree with him lesser, both intellectually and even morally. He also has almost no ability to self-reflect. While he can read other people's emotions quite effectively and is able to intellectually empathize, he can't actually feel their emotions. This allows him to operate "undercover" all while being ready and willing to destroy anyone who wounds his ego. While he suffers from a general lack of emotional self-control, he is emotionally and patiently strategic enough to set others up for his own gain.

When it comes to leadership, he is able to advance to high levels of position authority via manipulation, but he is seldom a leader who is loved. His colleagues placate him out of fear of retaliation or sheer exhaustion. He is more willing to be right to his own demise than wrong to his (or the company's) prosperity. He is classically the person who cuts his nose off to spite his face. Your ability to recognize him will help you succeed in many situations. EIPs are not the norm, but they are also not incredibly rare. Identifying their patterns and behaviors will allow you to see where they operate, but it will produce an even more useful outcome. The exaggerated behaviors of an EIP will shed light on a spectrum of healthy behaviors that many TPs and ATPs have, but which don't destructively cross the line as EIPs do.

Psychologists say there is such a thing as healthy narcissism. I'd debate that full assertion, but I do agree that there is a certain amount of confidence and self-agency that could be misconstrued as "healthy narcissism." If you don't recognize the difference between an EIP and an ATP with "healthy narcissism," you might promote the EIP due to what you think is his effectiveness and influence, when in reality, it is his manipulation and authority that got him his results. Often, EIPs treat their superiors with respect that they don't offer subordinates, thus making it difficult for the superior to see the way they treat others poorly. They manipulate others into agreeing with them, and then they make them do what they say but only due to their authority. This type of "leader" builds a compliant team, not a willing one. The more you raise their level of influence, by way of position in your organization, the more the culture will negatively transform and the more you'll be perceived as ignorant or hypocritical by other colleagues.

On the other hand, if you recognize EIP behaviors, you can identify the difference between them and other authentically influential people. Not all TPs and ATPs are easy to work with; therefore, inexperienced leaders may accidentally dismiss them as EIPs. This is a mistake because they are vastly different than the EIPs. TPs and ATPs have heavy opinions and will certainly push the limits of convincing others to go in certain directions, but they are self-reflective, and they do feel the emotions of others. This regulates them and tells them there is a point of diminishing returns on their pushing. The most important thing to keep in mind is that healthy people can have their bad moments and therefore act quite narcissistic. But this is fleeting. Whether it's stress, fatigue, or frustration, anyone can have a bad day. If you pay attention, you will be able to tell the difference.

THE BLINDING EFFECTS OF VICE

Often, organizations put committees together for good reason and they sometimes perform effectively. On other occasions, committees are formed to create the illusion of consensus. I was once on a church building committee. Part of the mission was to contemplate whether or not to tear down the old church when building a new one. The old church stood for over 150 years in a little town, so despite the obvious religious implications, it was a historical fixture of the community. The question was raised: Should we tear it down when we build a new church? Or should we keep it as a staple of what the community looked like, turning it into a bookstore, wedding venue, or the like, and simply build a completely new church adjacent to it? The committee chairman made it clear that he definitely wanted to tear the church down. To support his view, he claimed that "everyone" wanted to tear it down.

Noticing something was off, I pushed back, "I don't think so. I think some people may see it as a staple of the community."

"We've talked to everyone, and they all want it torn down," he claimed.

After going back and forth a bit, I suggested we do a professional survey of the parishioners and community. We did the survey, and sure enough, the results came back with a resounding 87% of people saying to *not* tear it down. Shockingly, at the next meeting, the chairman shared the results of the survey, with this assertion: "All right, as I said, everybody wants the church to be torn down."

I was dumbfounded. I was looking at the exact same survey, along with the other committee members, and it was clear that 87% of people did *not* want the church torn down. So, when I pointed out the obvious, this was the chairman's reply: "Exactly. The survey says 87% of those surveyed want the church to stay erect so we will take their counsel and tear it down." He wanted it torn down so badly that he was able to read statistics in direct opposition to reality just to pass his own agenda. Thankfully, this interpretation was reviled by the committee and the old church still stands today next to the new one.

When something like this happens, it feels like other agenda-driven power grabs, such as the "defund the police" movement, which made zero sense. Don't try to reason with an EIP. You can't use logic, reason, goodness, or justice when talking to an EIP. They know they are unfair and illogical. They use that strategy to confuse and frustrate you into submission. They are motivated by ego or power (one and the same). So, when negotiating or problem-solving with an EIP, be blunt about the fact that their agenda will not be tolerated.

Understanding the motives of EIPs requires diverting from the perspective seen in non-EIPs. This is where the "thinking like a criminal" connection is made. Before going there, remember your job isn't using your own biases to label someone or to believe that you can know for certain what motivates them. That lacks Justice. The purpose is to discern a potentially negative motive, which can enable you to preemptively eliminate possible negative outcomes.

For example, as a Giant who is mentally healthy, you are probably thinking about what is best for the organization and the people in it, around it, and impacted by it. That perspective will give you blind spots when talking to an EIP. Instead, to understand what motivates them, think, *If my only mission were to have power and respect, how would I act now? What decisions would I make? Who and what would be a threat to me?* This perspective will allow you to delicately navigate the landscape to avoid unnecessary conflict or to know when to assert your power and authority only because nothing else would work. Remember, lead with soft power whenever possible (i.e., influence), then, if that fails, don't refrain from using hard power. Asking those questions may also vindicate the other party from a negative false assumption. If they demonstrate behaviors that run counter to defending their ego, you are likely interacting with a TP or ATP who is having a weaker moment.

EIPs are often experienced and even competent professionals. In other words, they are good at their specific discipline. EIPs can be surgeons, pilots, and lawyers. However, they put organizations and individuals at risk whenever they are in positions of power because they can be erratic due to the subjective nature of ego. They are most dangerous when they are incompetent. When incompetent, they act like young children who say, "I want to do it myself," when helping dad or mom in the shop or kitchen. Children are not aware of the dangers of mom or dad letting go of a power tool or eggbeater. They think they are qualified to handle things when they aren't.

As a leader, you have to be prepared for times when somebody, for their own reasons of self-justification, will invert the truth to advance their own cause. EIPs believe they are the arbiters of truth. Facts do not matter to them; what they believe is true is true and they'll distort anything necessary to confirm it. They know that they're making you a bit crazy by trying to follow their logic. Gaslighting and stonewalling are classic weapons in their arsenal.

When someone does or says something that does not make sense, in an environment where rational analysis is supposed to be commonplace, we've identified that you need to look no further than ego in the EIP. However, a healthy TP or ATP can have a weak moment when self-justification or some other motivation like embarrassment overtakes them. This is why it's important to stay the course, keep an open mind, and observe behaviors over a period of time. It is a mistake to label people unfairly based on your own inexperience or errors of judgment. We all have a tendency to point fingers at others as a distraction from ourselves. So, constantly practice the Cardinal Virtues, assume the best in others, and be humble. Had I known this simple key to understanding human nature, many things in my earlier life would have turned out differently.

It's crucial not to assume your intuition is infallible and become judgmental as if you know the full reality all the time.

FIRE PASSIVE-AGGRESSIVE PEOPLE IMMEDIATELY

You can't work effectively with passive-aggressive people, yet we all have the potential to be passive-aggressive if pushed into the right circumstance. Passive-aggression is about assuming a false sense of power, and it often accompanies EIPs. When we feel powerless, we either do productive things to gain power or we do destructive things to feign it. One of the easiest and most immediate ways to gain power is passive-aggression. When people do this as a pattern in the workplace, they need to be let go. There is a difference between a liar and a person who has the potential to lie under duress. A liar lives by lies and uses them as a common means to an end, whereas the latter lives by truth but, as with all of us, has a human nature that is weak at times. The same holds true for passive-aggressive people versus others who can, if pushed too far, be passive-aggressive. That is why you need to look for patterns over time before you make a judgment.

Years ago, I had an employee who held the online passwords for several vendor accounts. As the company owner, I needed access to one of these accounts. When I asked for it, his response was, "You know what, I don't have that right now." This raised a red flag. When I pressed for a time frame, he said, "Well, I'll see when I can get it to you." Suddenly, I realized something was going on here. Why, as the owner, should I need to make an appointment for something so basic, something I have every right to access immediately, especially when there was no reasonable explanation for a delay?

In my experience, it usually takes only three instances in a short time frame to be sure if someone is passive-aggressive. An isolated act is probably not passive-aggressive in nature, just weakness in a bad moment. Passive-aggressive people have a pattern of using unmerited power to control others. A good example would be not replying to messages, gatekeeping, or hoarding resources without just cause. These people struggle in healthy relationships, which is why they will struggle working with you. In my experience, the time required for their transformation is rarely worth it. Some psychologists say you can't heal a narcissist, pedophile, or a pyromaniac. I'd be tempted to add passive-aggressive people to that list. While the grace of God can do miraculous things, in a practical work setting, it's more efficient to invest in finding, leading, and launching humble teammates who genuinely aspire to succeed.

Researchers examined how long it takes for a person to enter their car and leave a parking spot when someone is waiting for it.[1] Ideally, one would think to hurry up, knowing someone is waiting. Interestingly enough, it takes longer when someone is waiting. It's as if people think, *This parking spot is all I have that others want. Once I leave, I won't have anything enviable. So, I'm going to hold on to it as long as I can.* This study didn't target EIPs. It simply demonstrates that many people behave this way. It's important to consider that there could be factors or unusual circumstances causing behaviors that appear passive-aggressive. It's crucial not to assume your intuition is infallible and become judgmental as if you know the full reality, all the time.

After many years of experience, nine times out of ten, your intuition might be right. But it's arrogant to assume you're always right without investigating further. When you notice passive-aggressive behaviors, use your intuition and search for patterns. You may find a logical reason for the behavior. With enough experience, it's less likely to be wrong about these things. The hallmark of a Giant is leading others to develop virtue, all while becoming the best version of themselves. It's not to hold judgment over others without considering the possibility of being wrong.

GIANT TAKEAWAYS

There are three personality types that commonly interact with vice and virtue, leading to recognizable patterns of behavior:

1. **The Team Player (TP):** High-virtue, low-vice people who are interested in the best outcome for the company. They are well informed, humble, and interested.

2. **The Ambitious Team Player (ATP):** Torn between what is best for the company and what is best for themselves, they are political creatures who have a blend of virtuous behaviors and vice-oriented weak moments.

3. **The Egotistical Individual Player (EIP):** These people have almost no interest in what is good for the team unless it serves them. They have very low virtue, operate mostly from a vice-oriented perspective, and are either full-blown narcissists or exhibit heavy narcissistic tendencies.

Your ability to recognize the EIP will help you succeed in many situations. EIPs are not the norm, but they are also not incredibly rare. This type of "leader" builds a compliant team, not a willing one. The more you raise their level of influence, by way of position in your organization, the more the culture will negatively transform. Not all TPs and ATPs are easy to work with; therefore, inexperienced leaders may accidentally dismiss them as EIPs. This is a mistake because while TPs and ATPs have heavy opinions and will certainly push the limits of "convincing" others to go in certain directions, they are self-reflective, and they do feel the emotions of others.

As a Giant who is mentally healthy, you think about what is best for the organization and the people in it, around it, and impacted by it. That perspective will give you blind spots when talking to an EIP. Instead, to understand what motivates them, think, *If my only mission was to have power and respect, how would I act now? What decisions would I make? Who and what would be a threat to me?* When "thinking like a criminal," it's crucial not to assume your intuition is infallible and become judgmental as if you know the full reality, all the time.

17

How to Diagnose a Bad Culture

In a healthy organization, a strong culture acts like an immune system, naturally expelling the bad influences and retaining the good.

I n chapter 11, we discussed that simply maintaining a great culture isn't enough because cultures erode 1% a day unless you continuously repair and enhance them. It only takes 100 days of neglect to completely erode a great culture. That's why you must internally market your culture, recognize problems, and solve them at their root. Strengthening the core virtues that make it a great culture is necessary because all cultures are made or broken by vice or virtue. Therefore, it is crucial to know how to diagnose problems in your organization. Some are easier to identify than others. Production, manufacturing, distribution, and even sales leave data trails, but pounding data can lead some people to overlook the culture as the source. That approach often treats symptoms, not the disease. Ultimately, culture is the reason for most pervasive poor performances.

When a company's culture starts turning sour, you can usually find that it stems from one department and then spills out into another. Even though many people participate in cultural declines, ground zero usually starts with one individual or, in larger organizations, several individuals simultaneously. Ironically, the people who are most effective at eroding a culture appear warm, gregarious, and likable. Often, they appear vital to the team and have a bit of a cult following. People who influence others negatively tend to have traits such as self-justifying low performance. They find themselves underperforming, so they need to convince others the standards are too high. They often placate superiors. They act like they are happy at work and are "rising above the bad behaviors or performance of others." They are subtle complainers. They make slight comments about other departments to bolster their own value. You might hear them say, "I'm fine with what they do; it's just that it's not efficient [or any other descriptor]. But don't worry, I'll make up for what they lack." Finally, they want you to think that if they leave, others will follow. This is not something they generally say out loud, but they build loyal followers who seem to worship their opinion.

Here's a practical example of this happening. My lead directors mentioned an uptick in dissatisfaction by team members. There was a bit of petty infighting and sentiments from a few who said things like, "When will 'they' make this change?" A sign that a culture is either unhealthy or about to become unhealthy is "they" language. When team members see themselves as powerless and not on the same page as others, especially leaders, they separate themselves mentally by using "us" and "them" language. Pay attention to this pattern. Having experienced this type of thing in the past, I was motivated to help them identify the cause so we could make whatever corrections were necessary.

To eliminate any self-inflicted cultural errors, I asked questions centered on the virtue of Justice first, such as if there were any workload or standard changes that the departments may have recently implemented. It's important to first take stock of any potential responsibility on the organization's side of the equation. Giants don't point the finger at others with the assumption that their complaints or low morale are entirely their fault. After eliminating any changes from that angle, we began discussing the individuals closest to the situation. As we reviewed each person, I had an intuition about an employee we will call Jane. I pressed a bit further, asking more about her role. My intuition was heightened because the people closest to her had the most dissatisfaction in the company combined with low performance. This included one person quitting, a rare thing in our 2% voluntary turnover culture. They all glowed when talking about Jane. They went on saying, "She's the best one there. Everyone loves her. If she left, others would too. We've even asked her opinion on this, and she was very helpful." I acknowledged what they said, but since I sensed she might be part of the issue, I asked them to keep keen observations of the people she influenced most. They respectfully disagreed about her being part of the problem but agreed to keep their antennas up.

As time went on, the problems persisted and, eventually, Jane revealed her true colors. In the end, she was let go and, immediately, the culture improved. She was ground zero. The thing about these types of people is that they confuse others. They talk out of both sides of their mouths saying whatever serves them personally. It does take experience to recognize them, but the more you are aware of their type, the sooner you gain that experience and act on it.

It's important to differentiate this scenario from good people leaving a bad culture. That's an inverted situation. In healthy organizations, a strong culture acts like an immune system, naturally expelling the bad influences and retaining the good. An unhealthy culture retains negative influences and repels good people. When a valuable member leaves a culture and others go with them, it's a natural outcome. But, in a healthy culture with a destructive individual, it's generally a nano type who threatens to take people with him. In most situations, he fails, but if he does succeed, he usually takes weaker-minded team members who will likely be easily replaced anyway. One way to sniff out these cancerous people is by matching their negative attitudes to their low performance and the low performance in those they lead. As a reminder, don't just point a finger at them. Exhaust any possible role that you or other leaders may have had in unfairly putting a burden on them. If you falsely accuse or create an unfair situation, you will accelerate any existing decline in your culture.

THE UMBRELLA EFFECT

The previous example was about an employee who negatively impacted her peers. There is an even more important situation of which to be aware. That's when a leader shelters his or her department from the overall positive culture of the company at large. In other words, they put an umbrella over their team, insulating them from the rest of the organization. To a degree, Giants who lead departments will always bring their own flavor to the existing culture. This is a good thing if it is not counter to the general positive culture.

A leader who puts an umbrella over his group may say to you, the CEO, "Dave, my man, I just love working with you! You're such a great leader. So influential." But then, they go back to their team and say something like, "Just so you know, I don't agree with all of Dave's super high standards. Don't worry, I'm here to protect you from that. We all love Dave, but let's be honest, his expectations are unrealistic." It may take some time for that cancer to manifest fully, but when it does, it's a poison that will rot your company from the inside out.

I recall a low-performing CFO in one of my companies. It was earlier in my career as a CEO so, due to my lack of experience, he was able to hide his errors. His excuses for missing his own self-appointed deadlines and meetings piled up without any good explanation and the walls began closing in on him. I remember almost firing him on the spot when he said something remarkably revealing about himself: "I told my team that I am their advocate against the standards and expectations you have." I was stunned. As the CEO, I was on the side of *all* team members and departments. Telling his team that he is their advocate against me was incredibly divisive. He demonized me and my "high standards" while canonizing himself with the use of low standards and permissive capital.

In other words, he communicated the message that they can perform lazily and be protected from any harm that may come from big, bad Dave and his high standards. These are EIP behaviors like those I mentioned in the previous chapter. At the core was a passive-aggressive pattern of behavior. He blocked the overall healthy culture by putting an umbrella of low performance around his team, making all of them look bad to every other department. Needless to say, I fired him. Within two months, his replacement revamped the culture of the department. The ensuing result was high performance, low turnover, and high morale. The people under the umbrella of the new CFO fully integrated into the rest of the culture.

These situations might sound obscure, offbeat, or rare, but it is something I've seen happen often in many organizations. The difference between leading like a Giant with a great culture and leading like a nano in a bad culture isn't the absence of these situations. The difference is what you do to find these issues and how you act on them. Giants swiftly and fearlessly address cultural problems. Those who think this sort of thing doesn't happen in their organization are likely just overlooking it.

THE NUMBERS HELP YOU LEAD

If a team member refuses to track activity,
they are probably not doing the work.

Data is important in any business. If you don't measure your business activities, you can't monitor or understand expansion or retraction. One of the most important tools you will ever build will be a robust back office. Tracking sales data, consumer data, financial data, and other performance metrics is crucial. Beyond that, it is important to measure the performance standards, including how much time it takes to perform them. Here are a few real examples from companies:

- **Contract Data Entry:** *The average contract takes 4 minutes to enter and review before making it official. Therefore, an uninterrupted data entry person can perform 15 per hour. With reasonable breaks and collegial interaction, that should be a minimum of 12 but may be as high as 17.*

  This baseline tells you how many contracts a full- or part-time data entry person can and should do each day. When you include the cost of their salary and benefits, you can know how much their interaction with each sale impacts profit. Data entry is not a cost of goods sold; rather, it is an administrative expense. Despite that, you can now know that if you want to leverage growth/profit, you need to create a more streamlined data entry program so you can add more contracts in a shorter period with less employee interaction. It also tells you when someone is underperforming while giving them no room for excuses.

- **Collections Team:** *The average collections caller needs to make 4 calls to reach 1 client who is past due by 15 to 30 days. Clients who are between 30 and 60 days late require 5 calls on average, and clients past due beyond 60 days require 9 calls. The average duration of a call is 3 minutes.*

  This data tells you how much time each specialist needs to get the job done and whether or not to divide the specialists into different groups according to how late the client is in paying their bill. This data allows you to treat each specialist fairly by determining the different data points depending on what cohort they are calling.

- **Salespeople:** *The average time to generate 100 leads is 45 minutes. The number of calls required to get a decision-maker on the phone is 10. For every 10 decision-makers reached, 1 presentation is scheduled. Therefore, 100 calls produce 10 presentations. The average time to call 100 leads is 2.5 hours. Therefore, it takes 2.5 hours to get 10 presentations set. It takes a day to prepare for, travel to, and follow up on 2 presentations; therefore, 10 should be completed each week. The average closing percentage is 20%, and the average order size is $10,000. Therefore, it takes 1 week to make 2 sales for $20,000.*

  This data tells you how well salespeople perform, and it also tells you how to diagnose any reason for low or exceptional performance. If they are doing lots of appointments but not selling, it may be the quality of their presentation, lead qualification, closing skill, or conviction. If they aren't completing 10 appointments per week, it could be poor phone skills, motivation, commitment, outside stresses, belief in the opportunity, or many other factors.

These examples may or may not have direct application in your organization. Regardless, they show how having detailed data leads to transparency. Having data also allows you to have the corrective discussions required to build things to greater levels. Good data also prevents many excuses by objectively measuring things; however, it has its limitations too. Data is meant to be interacted with by leaders. Asking team members to gather data without reviewing your findings is lazy leadership. Giants use data to grow their business through thoughtful analysis and targeted correction.

FACTS ARE STUBBORN THINGS

Some of your greatest performers will be the most difficult to work with. Work with (most of) them anyway.

A major error that can be made when trying to diagnose problems in a culture that has gone sour is to think that a good culture is one that is always happy-go-lucky—one where everyone always gets along and there's no tension. That's not an accurate understanding of a healthy culture. Great cultures have healthy conflict, big personalities, and challenging days. Using "likability" and "easygoingness" to determine if someone is good or bad for a culture is a mistake. Some of the best team members come with the biggest opinions and challenges. The secret is to determine how those opinions and challenges impact the group as a whole.

I'm not the only sports fan to notice that huge personalities and big talent don't always equal a championship performance. Some highly talented athletes have so much personal drama or self-centered behavior associated with them that they prevent the team they are on from jelling. Yet other big personalities, with strong opinions, know when too much is too much. They have a unique way of inspiring people, including those people who find them a bit off-putting. Here's the primary way to tell the difference between the two. A difficult person who is a valuable team player, no matter how much he pushes issues, he does it for the good of the team. He is sincere, albeit a bit much to handle. On the other hand, the person who is difficult and self-serving pushes for his own ambition, so he has got to go. At times these people manifest by how they deny facts and other forms of reality. This usually begins in their personal lives but spills into the way they make organizational decisions.

Prideful, ambitious people are easily deceived by childlike, silly, and dangerous ideas, including those that are recycled for centuries. Semi-modern philosophers like Descartes and Kant have negatively influenced academia. Stemming from their philosophy, students are taught the idea that everyone can have their own truth. When a professor, who has no immediate practical consequences for teaching lies, deceives students, it's one thing. But for leaders who are held accountable for results, the truth matters. You want your surgeon to know the objective truth that determines your right arm from your left and your heart from your kidney? As I wrote in chapter 5, saying there is no such thing as truth is a pervasive fallacy. It has been repeated throughout history, albeit presented differently from generation to generation. It is said that to free a person from their human nature, we have a conscience built into it.

We can't all have our own truth. We can have our own perception of truth, but if that perception is not in line with what's actually true, then your perception of truth is simply wrong. Expanding on a point I mentioned earlier in the book, if I like tomatoes, that's a fact; it's not "my truth." If someone else believes I don't like tomatoes, their "truth" doesn't change the fact that I do. There is a concrete truth—I like tomatoes—and no belief or perspective can alter that reality. We must choose to either accept the truth (I like tomatoes) or embrace a falsehood (I don't like tomatoes).

In the context of hiring, I firmly believe in avoiding individuals who deny the existence of absolute truths. If there is no such thing as an absolute truth, then the declaration "there is no such thing as absolute truth" absolutely can't be true. Anyone who can't follow that logic is not qualified to make important decisions. If someone thinks that flawed thinking won't show up in their HR office at some point, they're a bit naive. In a professional setting, you can't afford to have decision-makers who don't acknowledge objective truths. You need clarity and reality from your team, or else you'll wind up with a bad culture in need of diagnosis.

GIANT TAKEAWAYS

When a company's culture starts turning sour, you can usually find that it stems from one department, and ground zero usually starts with one individual. Here are ways to sniff them out, just like a keen-nosed dog can identify disease.

These people:

- appear warm, gregarious, and likable, but are ironically the most effective at eroding a culture.
- appear vital to the team and have a bit of a cult following.
- often placate superiors.
- act like they are happy at work and are "rising above the bad behaviors or performance of others."
- are subtle complainers.
- want you to think that if they leave, others will follow.

In healthy organizations, a strong culture acts like an immune system, naturally expelling the bad influences and retaining the good. An unhealthy culture retains negative influences and repels good people. When a valuable member leaves a culture and others go with them, it's a natural outcome.

Watch out for the Umbrella Effect, which is when a leader shelters his or her department from the overall positive culture of the company at large. In other words, they put an umbrella over their team, insulating them from the rest of the organization. These people will be pleasant to your face but villainize you the moment you're not around. The easy way to spot the Umbrella Effect is that there will be low performance and low morale all around these EIP types. So, avoid hiring or retaining EIP individuals who are passive-aggressive, judgmental, dishonest, lazy, and especially those who reject the concept of absolute truth. Why? Because you can try to succeed in spite of them, but you can never build a good culture with them.

18

Know Who You Are and What You Stand For

Be vigilant against political, social, and cultural BS that will interfere with your pursuit of what is right and good.

---

once visited a large Fortune 100 company where they asked me to conduct a seminar for a large division. They mentioned the need to develop a theme for the meeting, which is good practice. As the discussion ensued, I realized they were trying to create more than just a theme. At each annual meeting they were trying on a new culture, and it raised a red flag. I asked for examples of past themes, and they listed *Good to Great*, *Who Moved My Cheese?*, and *Eat That Frog!*, all of which were great books but none of which stuck in a practical sense. As I listened, I gained insight into some of their problems; it became clear that this large division had no distinct culture of its own while simultaneously ignoring the overall company culture. Instead, they were trying to implement culture based on the latest popular book or trend. They would introduce a book, distribute copies, use it as a cultural theme for a seminar, and then move on.

All of these books would have been great to share as part of an existing healthy culture, but without one already in place, the themes could not be planted, watered, and harvested. Without a solid underlying culture, their efforts were not only futile, but kept them perpetually distracted from creating something they could actually build upon. Like many companies, they were like seaweed, drifting with the current. They would observe the overall climate and, upon identifying a problem, attempt to correct it with the latest trend, treating a symptom but not the disease. True leadership is like being a stump in the water. Most of the time it's unglamorous, but unyielding and steadfast, the stump is immovable regardless of the water's direction.

When people lead and make decisions like seaweed, bad things happen. If you conduct market research to identify certain demographics, great. But when you use themes, polls, marketing trends, or public opinions as an overarching leadership strategy, it's never going to work because these things inherently change. Leadership is about enacting principles that stand the test of time, and constantly refining them as you personally evolve and grow professionally. When there's a growing sentiment because of a new trend or popular political/social idea, nanos will go along with it, hoping it will yield higher profits and greater productivity, or to virtue signal conscientiousness. If you want to market your product to certain demographics based on trends, go ahead, but beware.

This caution is on both sides of the spectrum. And while I clearly have opinions about these matters, my take on this is more about leadership than being on the right or the left. What do Nike, Levi's, Target, Capital One, and Bud Light all have in common? Trials and tribulations due to getting involved in political stances on one side or the other. Bud Light took hits on both the left and right sides of the chin. On one side, the brand faced a major backlash in 2023 due to collaborating with a controversial transgender TikTok influencer. Intending to reach the LGBT community, Anheuser-Busch, the company behind Bud Light, overlooked their conservative beer-drinking customers. The situation escalated with people posting videos of themselves destroying Bud Light products, leading to an unprecedented boycott of all Anheuser-Busch products. When trying to reconcile its conservative customer base, they made a hard pivot in advertising, featuring uber-patriotic imagery and their world-renowned Clydesdale horses. In this attempt to distance themselves from controversy, Anheuser-Busch took a hit on other side when they faced a secondary boycott from the LGBT community. The entire situation made a mockery of the company, highlighting the pitfalls of going along with social and political ideas. As a result, Bud Light's sales plummeted, and their brand image was tarnished. I fail to recall a better, or worse, example of bending to current trends or public opinions leading to disastrous consequences for a brand.

Going along with contemporary movements will never win in the long term, and it will leave both your customers and employees unsatisfied.

It is one thing for a company to sell a product to a target market. Humans typically respect people with different beliefs and recognize that certain products are classically "different strokes for different folks." The problem comes when they try to force their beliefs on others. Had Bud Light chosen to show a big party filled with all sorts of people, including a transgender person in the crowd, most people would have looked past it as a snapshot of the moment. But deliberately going out of their way to make a big statement is taking a stand for something that also happens to be against something. The crazy thing is: none of it has anything to do with beer! The protest came from telling the beer drinker what he should value.

I'm not saying that a company doesn't have the right to promote their product any way they want. I'm simply saying that, most often, taking these stances in marketing is a view not worth the climb. In matters of political and social movements, it's best to stay away from them altogether. It's unrealistic that every single person at your company, and the customers you serve, share the same beliefs. If you jump on the latest popular political trend, left or right, and then force it upon your consumers, you risk losing business. A church or political group will "sell" a stance because that stance is central to what they offer, but most products have nothing to do with these stances.

My Neville Chamberlain attitude about companies picking target markets as they see fit turns into a more guarded attitude when it comes to the internal workings of an organization. Promoting and forcing polarized views on team members who don't share beliefs is counterproductive. Inherently, this approach doesn't satisfy customers or unify employees. You risk alienating half of your employees, which means that the organization will be running on half power. When they go home and have pillow talk, they'll be saying what they really feel about the company.

"Go woke or go broke," as Mark Cuban promotes, is shortsighted. Sure, some companies do well in that environment. Some even prosper. But the backlash is real and growing. "No woke" recruiting sites are building fast and droves of employees are leaving woke businesses to work for companies that promote conservative ideas. Companies that do so will also face a similar but opposite backlash. Again, this is the right of both sides. The problem I see is that choosing to have a left-leaning or right-leaning company is a new phenomenon. It's not a necessary choice when it comes to internal issues unless the product or service is related to something that is agenda driven. How in the world is ice cream a left or right product?

How is a credit card a left or right product? Why does a shoe have to tell me what I need to value? These stances are artificially induced.

If I entered my business insisting that everyone must accept my values or be canceled, I'd be a dictator, not a leader. It's one thing to express my beliefs when asked about them, respecting whether someone agrees or not. But it's entirely different, and harmful, to demand conformity to beliefs. If you do this, you won't build a team of Giants; you'll just drive everyone crazy.

A true leader is not the one with the most minions, but the one who creates the most Giants.

BE THE STUMP, NOT SEAWEED

A leader, and an organization, should have the freedom to say whatever they want. As a result, some people will follow, and other people won't want to be around them. That's their choice. But when someone invites you into an idea, you're going to respect that person far more than someone who forces you to accept a belief or idea you think is false. Even if someone whom you report to has very different beliefs, as long as they don't show you disrespect or demand that you comply with their agenda, you're probably willing to follow them. Influence, not force, is what creates long-term success.

The goal of a successful organization is to build something meaningful. Being united and working toward something good generally has nothing to do with agendas or what someone likes to do on the weekend. The purpose of business is simple: create a product, sell it at a fair price to those who need it, and do so with integrity while creating just opportunities for your employees and contributing positively to the community.

This common mission transcends personal preference regarding most of the political issues that enter the workplace. Most company missions have nothing to do with popular trends; they are about working together toward something good, true, and beautiful. If your organization is not central to a cause, as soon as you start throwing in any sort of political garbage, regardless of however justified it seems, you won't get anywhere. All you'll do is confuse your people.

People want freedom in the workplace, not tyranny. Tyranny forces someone to praise something they don't value. When you make people declare a value they don't actually have, it's going to cause harm. If you value something like the Cardinal Virtues or the Transcendentals, others may be inclined to value it also but you can't make them. Likewise, you can't declare, "We believe in diversity, equity, and inclusion," and then force people to say out loud what they believe. You can't force people to value and believe things. As soon as you force them to, no matter what kind of victory you think you've won, you haven't because they'll despise you for it.

People resent tyrannical leaders, leading to a lack of enthusiasm for work and a reluctance to contribute positively. On the other hand, an empathetic leader creates a culture of strength, freedom, and unity. In that environment, self-serving agendas and egotistic behaviors don't thrive. As I've said, a strong organizational culture is like an immune system: it either assimilates individuals, helping them grow, or expels those who don't align with its values. To lead organizations, you must do it according to proven principles, not political or social ideas. Introducing socially charged issues into the workplace is often an attempt by individuals to gain authority or legitimacy. However, this is a form of subtle tyranny, as it serves their personal agenda under the guise of addressing real issues like racism, discrimination, or unprofessional treatment.

Above all, you need strength to lead. And there is no strength in going along with what's popular, incorporating it into your marketing strategy, and making it a part of your leadership philosophy and company culture. That doesn't make any sense at all. Just because something becomes popular, it doesn't mean that you should implement it. Be resolute in your commitment to creating something extraordinary, regardless of the elite, political, or social BS.

A SURPRISING WAY TO GUARD YOUR CULTURE

*When you talk to a team member,
keep their pillow talk in mind.*

If you require people in your organization to say or partake in things they don't believe in, they're going to resent you. At the end of the day, when people lay their head on the pillow next to the person they love, they may be inclined to say something about you or your organization. In the most intimate setting, is what they say good or bad? No matter what the reason, if your people go home and complain every day, their friends and family are going to tell them to quit. Even if the complaints aren't justified, having friends and family working against you hampers your ability to train, retain, or launch them to higher levels of success.

Of course, you shouldn't be obsessive about what other people say because you have to be willing to assume the pillow talk will be negative sometimes. The strategy for managing pillow talk is simple: when you must have a hard conversation with somebody, or talk to somebody who disagrees with you, treat them fairly and with kindness. A pillow talk victory in this regard sounds like this: "Dave wants to go in this particular direction, and I don't like it. In fact, I disagreed with him in a meeting. Even though I don't like it, he respected my position, and I appreciated it." That's an important victory.

In the introduction to section 3, I said that a great detective has to think like a criminal and a great leader has to think like an excuse-maker. When consulting with somebody who wanted to get into the Airbnb business, I told him that to be effective he needed to manage online reviews because they impact occupancy dramatically. "How do you do that?" he asked. I told him that he has to imagine that he's the guest. I told him to go into the home as if he didn't know or even care about the owner. I encouraged him to be extreme about it, behaving as if this is the one trip he'd take all year, and to look for every single way he might complain. When you grab the door handle, open the fridge, try to find the remote, and step in the shower, etc., how do you feel? By doing this, you correct things before they have the potential to cause problems. The next pieces of advice were important, but not even close to the priority of doing everything possible to guard against the guest laying their head down at night, fuming with all the things wrong with their stay and taking it out on the owner by way of reviews.

When it comes to leading teams, conflict and perceptions of injustice will flare up. Let's say you have to tell a person they're not receiving a promotion. When you do, it's best to imagine every objection they're going to have to your stance. Ask yourself, "How is a person with a wounded ego going to spin this when they go home and talk to their spouse?" On one occasion, I needed to demote an employee who was derelict in the leadership portion of his "player coach"-type role. On the player side, he excelled, so I wanted to retain him in that capacity. When I spoke to him about the reasons why, he could not debate them. I used data and many concrete examples to make my point. He knew that if he debated my decision, I could have pulled out many more objective examples. Being armed with reasons but choosing not to use all of them is a good way for someone to recognize that you are sparing his dignity. During the course of the discussion and prior to me officially stripping him of the role, he interrupted and asked me if it would be okay for him to tell his wife that the decision to step down from leadership was his own. The timing worked and I agreed. That is a good example of how this sort of thing can go well but otherwise could have gone poorly.

As often as possible, structure the conversation so it leads them to make a decision on their own in the face of an inevitably negative outcome. People like to make their own choices even if it includes knowing it will be made for them if they don't do it on their own. This, to a cynic, might seem manipulative, but compassion, not dominance, is the motive, and the subject knows it. By getting ahead of things, you're preserving their self-esteem as best you can amid awkward moments.

Keeping the pillow talk in mind is synonymous with taking preventative action for the good of everyone. There are countless small, everyday examples of using preemptive emotional management strategies. Imagine a small business scenario where there are 10 people in a department, and only two of them ever use the break room. The business is growing, and the room is needed for expansion. If you were to announce that you're planning to get rid of the break room because "nobody uses it," eight of them would readily agree since they don't use it. However, the two individuals who do use it may understandably be upset. From their perspective, it would seem like you referred to them as "nobodies" by saying that "nobody uses it." That might create unnecessary drama in the workplace and bad pillow talk when they get home.

Before conducting a group meeting to let the department know of the change, it would be best to take the time to have one-on-one conversations with those two individuals. Say something like, "Hey, Katie, I know how much you value the break room and use it regularly. However, from a growth standpoint, we can't keep it. I know that might be disappointing, but we need the space for other purposes. If there were a way that I could keep it, I would. But this really is the only way we can expand in this space. Sorry about the inconvenience. I wanted to let you know before I told the rest of the team out of respect."

In response, a reasonable person would likely say, "Thank you for considering me. I appreciate that you see my concerns are valid." So, how does that pillow talk sound? It usually sounds like this: "Dave was really nice about it. He gets that I used the break room often. But he was respectful about getting rid of it, and he even noticed that I used it." One huge aspect of considering pillow talk isn't to make things perfect for everybody so they go home and only say great things. Sometimes you have to give people a hard pill to swallow, but always consider the impact.

Many years ago, one of my businesses needed to move to a new location due to rapid growth. Prior to the move, our young startup company had hodgepodge furniture because we were bootstrapping our way to profit. The furniture was mismatched and relatively sloppy and departments were on top of each other. When we made the move, we invested in new furniture and had an award-winning designer help create what ended up being another award-winning space. The new office reflected our growth and would be used for more client interaction. We anticipated the move might be challenging for some employees because change is difficult for some people even when it is positive. The new location had specifically designed spaces that allowed department workflows to be more efficient and creative. This meant some employees would be sitting in different proximity to colleagues than they did in the old location. We knew this would probably not be a problem for most because, despite new seating arrangements, we had collective workspaces throughout so every employee could work wherever they wanted for the most part. As petty as it may sound, despite having high morale and an incredible team and culture, some employees were not happy with new seating arrangements. It would have been very easy to assume that, since the team was so resilient, these things wouldn't have mattered but I coached our leaders to "think like a criminal" and "keep pillow talk in mind."

On moving day, as we all settled into our sleek and modern new office, there was an atmosphere of excitement and pride for nearly all 100 or so employees at the time. However, one employee moved from her newly assigned space to be next to her boyfriend, who was in a completely unrelated department. She was a great team member, but in this moment she was defiant. She was having a difficult emotional time with the change. Her supervisor made it clear that she needed to work in the new space and that she and her boyfriend could work in the communal areas whenever it was practical. This wasn't good enough for her and eventually she quit. No preventative work could have saved her from herself.

On the other hand, another employee had a few issues with things she disliked, and she stepped out angrily to call her husband to complain (a daytime version of pillow talk). Within minutes, she came back in and apologized. Because her normal dialogue with him was positive regarding her work experience, he helped her see the perspective from our side and advocated for her supervisor. She continued to be an exemplary team member who was promoted several times. This serves as a great example of how even the most reasonable people can sometimes get something silly stuck in their heads. This is true about them, you, and me. It's important to get ahead of these things when possible. When you've built a positive work atmosphere and a history of fairness, you can be confident that your decisions will most often be respected.

BRINGING IT ALL HOME

When people go home and have pillow talk, they're going to say, "That was unfair," or "That was fair"—Justice. They are going to say, "I'm so motivated," or "I couldn't be more done with that hellhole"—Fortitude. "I'm afraid of losing my job for what I did," or "I'm ready to face the consequences"—also Fortitude. "I want to say this hurtful thing to this other person," or "I'm going to guard the culture"—Temperance.

Most people can sense injustice when they are subject to it, even if they might understand Justice enough to deliver it. Even if they wouldn't be able to articulate what the Transcendentals are, they will be drawn to unity, truth, beauty, and goodness. What often upsets us about others is a reflection of what we are capable of seeing in ourselves. If you watch someone be rude to a cashier, you could judge them for it, bad-mouthing them to the cashier when it's your turn in line. Or, when you speak to the cashier, you can empathize with them both, saying, "Wow, he must be having a hard day. I'm sorry he treated you like that." If you have this perspective, you see it from the level of empathy, which yields connection, not judgment, which just furthers separation. The ability to recognize virtues is the same; if you see something that's prudent, that means you know what Prudence in action looks like. The goal, therefore, is to develop your ability to not just look for it but live it.

Another reason you should want to build the Cardinal Virtues is that, without them, you are a sitting duck to be manipulated. The more you've personally grasped Prudence, Justice, Fortitude, and Temperance, the easier it is to spot bad behaviors. Inevitably, there will be people who try to manipulate you, but when you practice the Cardinal Virtues, you will see them coming. Without virtue, people can influence you to make bad decisions. The only way to lead with confidence and withstand the tests of weak people is to develop in virtue. This makes you a master of influence, rarely needing to use force to take people where they need and want to go.

GIANT TAKEAWAYS

- Don't be like seaweed, drifting with the current. When identifying a problem, correct it at the source, not with the latest trend.
- Going along with contemporary movements will never win in the long term, and it will leave both your customers and employees unsatisfied.

- If you insist that everyone must accept your values or be canceled, you'll be a dictator, not a leader. If you do this, you won't build a team of Giants; you'll just drive everyone crazy.

- The purpose of business is simple: create a product, sell it at a fair price to those who need it, and do so with integrity, all while creating opportunities for your employees and contributing positively to the community.

- An empathetic leader creates a culture of strength, freedom, and unity. In this environment, self-serving agendas and egotistic behaviors will not thrive.

- When you must have a hard conversation, or talk to somebody who disagrees with you, treat them fairly and with kindness. This will lead to people having good pillow talk, making them ready and refreshed to come back to work.

The following exercise will help you self-reflect on your understanding and implementation of the Cardinal Virtues—the most straightforward way to master influence and become a Giant:

Personal Definition	**Application**
Prudence is . . .	I'd become more prudent by . . .
Prudence is not . . .	I'd become more just by . . .
Justice is . . .	I'd become more fortified by . . .
Justice is not . . .	I'd become more temperate by . . .
Fortitude is . . .	**Integration:** Consider a situation where each virtue was tested.
Fortitude is not . . .	Prudence:
Temperance is . . .	Justice:
Temperance is not . . .	Fortitude:
	Temperance:

CONCLUSION

Only Giants can lead Giants. Thankfully, being a Giant is more of a journey than a destination. In the process of committing to and perfecting yourself in virtue, you'll be drawn to lead others to do the same. The more you advance in self-mastery, the bigger you become, until you see head and shoulders above the crowd. Yet it's clear leaders carry a unique burden. They are guardians, protectors, providers, judges, helpers, servants, counselors, and friends—*and only a Giant can be all of those at one time.*

The most tragic thing I have witnessed in my 35-plus years of leadership is when someone fails to recognize the potential they have inside. While some people fail due to excessive pride, most people sit on the sidelines of life and bury their talents due to apathy or a lack of confidence. If someone were capable of living a perfect life, you'd see that they never squandered any potential, ever. Since none of us are perfect, we all have potential that goes unused. To what degree we leave that potential untouched is the degree that we will have dissatisfaction. So, then, we are meant to test the limits of our greatness by trusting that we were made for more.

I was asked by a young man to summarize what it means to me, at the most personal level, to be a Giant. My answer may not be the same as yours, but to me, it is simple. It's to be face-to-face with God hearing the words, "Well done, good and faithful servant. You invested your talents wisely and didn't bury a single one."

ELEVATE YOUR LEADERSHIP - MASTER YOUR INFLUENCE - NETWORK WITH GIANTS

Subscribe to my YouTube channel (Dave Durand) and follow me on LinkedIn so we can be Giants and slay dragons together.

Also join the

LEADING GIANTS MASTERCLASS

As you've now turned the last page of this book, your journey to excellence is just beginning. The insights you've gained are a solid foundation, and now it's time to build upon them! With the Leading Giants Masterclass, you get:

1. A comprehensive library of over 100 online course modules, tailored worksheets, and evaluations designed to translate knowledge into actionable, real-world strategies.
2. The chance to enhance your learning with coaching sessions, providing the mentorship and accountability crucial for growth in entrepreneurship, leadership, and sales mastery.
3. To become part of an exclusive community in the Giants Networking Group, where new connections and opportunities with other Giants await you! Plus, you gain access to extended podcast interviews and content featuring exclusive insights from industry leaders.

The path to becoming a Giant in your field started by reading this book, but your success will be made possible through this Masterclass. Visit www.leadinggiants.com to take your first step today.

ACKNOWLEDGMENTS

I want to thank my colleagues at Best Version Media LLC and Leading Giants LLC for their support and encouragement of this project.

Special thanks to Syris King-Klem for keeping the project on task and contributing to the writing process in the most profound way.

To my parents and children, who have taught me countless lessons, and to my beautiful wife, Miranda, who inspires and encourages me to slay dragons like no one else could: I love you.

All glory to God, for all the gifts and treasures that He has given, none of which I deserve.

ENDNOTES

CHAPTER 1

1. Dave Durand, *Perpetual Motivation: How to Light Your Fire and Keep It Burning in Your Career and in Life* (ProBalance Incorporated, 2000).
2. Aristotle, *Nicomachean Ethics*.
3. Josef Pieper, *The Four Cardinal Virtues: Human Agency, Intellectual Traditions, and Responsible Knowledge* (University of Notre Dame Press, 1990).

CHAPTER 2

1. Eden King, Lisa Finkelstein, Courtney Thomas, and Abby Corrington, "Generational Differences at Work Are Small. Thinking They're Big Affects Our Behavior," *Harvard Business Review*, August 1, 2019, https://hbr.org/2019/08/generational-differences-at-work-are-small-thinking-theyre-big-affects-our-behavior.
2. Sara McLanahan and Gary Sandefur, *Growing Up with a Single Parent* (Harvard University Press, 1997).
3. D. A. Dawson, "Family Structure and Children's Health and Well-Being: Data from the 1988 National Health Interview Survey on Child Health," *Journal of Marriage and the Family* 53, no. 3 (1991): 573–584.
4. Peter Hill, "Recent Advances in Selected Aspects of Adolescent Development," *Journal of Child Psychology and Psychiatry* 34, no. 1 (January 1993): 69–99.

5. "Data and Statistics on Children's Mental Health | CDC," Centers for Disease Control and Prevention, June 3, 2022, https://www.cdc.gov/childrensmentalhealth/data.html.
6. National Center on Substance Abuse and Child Welfare, "Number of Children Who Entered Out of Home Care with Parental Alcohol or Drug Abuse as a Condition Associated with Removal, by Age in the United States, 2021," n.d., https://ncsacw.acf.hhs.gov/research/child-welfare-statistics/interactive-statistics-series/7-enter-out-of-home-care-age-at-removal-aod/.
7. "Children in Single-Parent Households," County Health Rankings & Roadmaps, n.d., https://www.countyhealthrankings.org/health-data/health-factors/social-economic-factors/family-and-social-support/children-in-single-parent-households?year=2024.
8. "If I Could: Families Destroy Themselves, so Families Have to Heal Themselves | Office of Justice Programs," n.d., https://www.ojp.gov/ncjrs/virtual-library/abstracts/if-i-could-families-destroy-themselves-so-families-have-heal.
9. Sara McLanahan and Larry Bumpass, "Intergenerational Consequences of Family Disruption," *American Journal of Sociology* 95, no. 1 (July 1988): 130–152.
10. Ben Kesling, "The U.S. Military's Weight Challenge: 'Skinny-Fat' Recruits," MSN, Oct 1, 2023, https://www.msn.com/en-us/health/other/the-u-s-military-s-weighty-challenge-skinny-fat-recruits/ar-AA1hwgbw.

CHAPTER 5

1. American Worldview Inventory 2020, reported by Arizona Christian University Cultural Research Center.
2. Kristen Weir, "Nurtured By Nature," *Monitor on Psychology* 51, no. 3 (April 1, 2020), https://www.apa.org/monitor/2020/04/nurtured-nature.

CHAPTER 6

1. Frank Dobbin and Alexandra Kalev, "Why Diversity Programs Fail and What Works Better," *Harvard Business Review*, March 27, 2024, https://hbr.org/2016/07/why-diversity-programs-fail.

2. Zach Jewell, "Ben Shapiro Sits Down with Elon Musk for Exclusive Wide-Ranging Discussion on DEI, Space, Religion," *Daily Wire*, January 24, 2024, https://www.dailywire.com/news/ben-shapiro-sits-down-with-elon-musk-for-exclusive-wide-ranging-discussion-on-dei-space-religion.

3. U.S. Census Bureau, "Census Project Shows Job Flows by Institution, Degree, Major and Geography," Census.gov, October 28, 2021, https://www.census.gov/library/stories/2019/08/where-do-college-graduates-go-for-jobs.html.

4. Traci Pedersen, "The 4 Temperaments: Understanding Choleric Temperament," Psych Central, February 12, 2024, https://psychcentral.com/health/choleric-temperament#4-temperaments.

CHAPTER 8

1. Josef Pieper, *Leisure, the Basis of Culture* (Ignatius Press, 2009).

CHAPTER 11

1. Tamara J. Erickson and Lynda Gratton, "What It Means to Work Here," *Harvard Business Review*, August 1, 2014, https://hbr.org/2007/03/what-it-means-to-work-here.

CHAPTER 13

1. Shahram Heshmat, "Five Ways Music Can Empower You," *Psychology Today*, September 12, 2022, https://www.psychologytoday.com/gb/blog/science-choice/202209/5-ways-music-can-empower-you.

CHAPTER 16

1. Alexis C. Madrigal, "Science: People Really Do Take Longer Leaving a Parking Spot When You Are Waiting for It," *The Atlantic*, February 18, 2011, https://www.theatlantic.com/technology/archive/2011/02/science-people-really-do-take-longer-leaving-a-parking-spot-when-youre-waiting-for-it/71439/.

ABOUT THE AUTHOR

Dave Durand is the CEO of Leading Giants where he and his team coach leaders to maximize influence and grow their companies. He is a co-founder and past CEO of Best Version Media where he remains the Executive Chairman. Additionally, he has built and sold several businesses with over a billion dollars in combined sales. Dave is married to Miranda and together they have nine children.